MILAN &
THE ITALIAN LAKES

BY
BARBARA AND STILLMAN ROGERS

Produced by
Thomas Cook Publishing

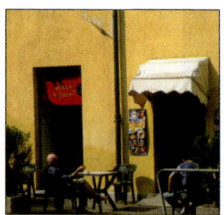

Written by Barbara and Stillman Rogers

Original photography by Stillman Rogers
Original design by Laburnum Technologies Pvt Ltd

Editing and page layout by Cambridge Publishing Management Limited,
149B Histon Road, Cambridge CB4 3JD

Published by Thomas Cook Publishing
A division of Thomas Cook Tour Operations Limited

PO Box 227, The Thomas Cook Business Park, Unit 15/16,
Coningsby Road, Peterborough PE3 8SB, United Kingdom
E-mail: books@thomascook.com
www.thomascookpublishing.com

ISBN: 1-841573-88-4

Text © 2004 Thomas Cook Publishing
Maps © 2004 Thomas Cook Publishing
First edition © 2004 Thomas Cook Publishing

Head of Thomas Cook Publishing: Donald Greig
Project Editor: Charlotte Christensen
Project Administration: Michelle Warrington
DTP: Steven Collins

All rights reserved. No part of this publication may be reproduced, stored in a retrieval system or transmitted, in any form or by any means, electronic, mechanical, recording or otherwise, in any part of the world, without prior permission of the publisher. Requests for permission should be addressed to Thomas Cook Publishing, PO Box 227, The Thomas Cook Business Park, Units 15–16, Coningsby Road, Peterborough PE3 8SB, United Kingdom.

Although every care has been taken in compiling this publication, and the contents are believed to be correct at the time of printing, Thomas Cook Tour Operations Limited cannot accept any responsibility for errors or omissions, however caused, or for changes in details given in the guidebook, or for the consequences of any reliance on the information provided.

The opinions and assessments expressed in this book do not necessarily represent those of Thomas Cook Tour Operations Limited.

Printed and bound in Spain by: Grafo Industrias Gráficas, Basauri

Cover: The town of Torbole on Lake Garda. Photograph by Charles Bowman/Robert Harding World Imagery
Inside cover: All photos by Brand X Pictures/Alamy, except bottom left by ImageGap/Alamy

CD manufacturing services provided by business interactive ltd, Rutland, UK.
CD edited and designed by Laburnum Technologies Pvt Ltd

Contents

background	4–17
Introduction	4
Land and People	6
History	8
Governance	10
Culture	14
Festivals and Events	16

first steps	18–23

what to see	24–151
Milan	24
Casa del Manzoni	30
Lake Maggiore	52
Lago d'Orta	66
Lago di Lugano	70
Lake Como	76
Isola Comacina	86
Bergamo	92
Lago d'Iseo	102
Brescia	106
Lago di Garda	112
Verona	132
Mantova	144

directory	152–89
Shopping	152
Entertainment	154
Children	158
Sport and Leisure	160
Food and Drink	164
Hotels and Accommodation	172
Practical Guide	178

index	190–91

Features

Rome in Northern Italy	12
Travelling by Boat and Train	22
Castello Sforzesco	26
Milan's Architecture	32
The Borromeo Family	60
Agri-tourism	90
The Venetian Empire: Looking for Lions	98
Il Vittoriale	116
The Risorgimento and the Red Cross	148
Opera, Opera Everywhere	156
Savouring Local Wines	170
Living in a Villa	176

Walks/Train/Boat/Driving Tours

Walk: The Duomo	28
Walk: Central Milan	40
Train and Boat Tour: Lake Como from Milan	46
Excursion: Monza	48
Driving Tour: Val d'Aosta	50
Boat Tour: Borromean Islands	56
Excursion: Lake Varese	64
Boat Tour: Lake Lugano	72
Train Tour: Centovalli	74
Excursion: San Pellegrino and the Val Brembana	100
Walk: Brescia	110
Driving Tour: Lake Idro Route	128
Excursion: Rovereto	130
Walk: Old Verona	140
Excursion: The Valpolicella Region	142
Driving Tour: Along the River Mincio	150

background

Introduction

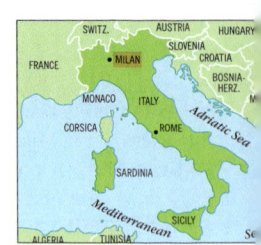

Say you are going to Italy and everyone is envious. This land of sunshine, Campari and *La Dolce Vita* is at the top of everyone's list. Say you are going to the lakes and Milan, and you immediately become a sophisticated traveller. Clearly you are eschewing the ever-popular Golden Triangle of Rome–Florence–Venice because you have already been there.

Perhaps you have visited Italy before, or perhaps this is your first trip. It doesn't matter. This is a good place to begin, and a good a place to come back to. Nowhere in Italy – or all of Europe – can claim better scenery than the snow-covered Alps reflected in the deep blue waters of a lake whose steep shores are dotted with pastel-coloured buildings. When these wooded mountain sides give way to soaring rock cliffs, and little white sailing boats drift back and forth in the water below, the view only improves.

Northern Italy is a cultural paradise, with enough music (from grand opera to jazz), museums, *palazzi* (palaces), art galleries, monumental buildings and fashion design to gratify the most dedicated patron. Its churches are museums in their own right, showcases of architectural styles, historic treasures and works by famous artists.

The Lakes Region is relatively small, with good transportation. Travellers can go from the fashion streets of Milan to a home-grown

Pastel towns cluster along the steep lake shores

background

celebration of a fruit harvest in the most rural of mountain villages, all in the same day. They can begin a lazy morning lingering over a cappuccino in a café overlooking Milan's Duomo (cathedral), hop on a train to Como for a scenic boat tour of the lake and be back in Milan in time to change for dinner – or dine beside Lake Como and take a later train.

At the heart of any traveller's experiences in Lombardy is their willingness to join local people in their traditions. This might be simply going to church in a local parish or choosing the little *trattoria* instead of a famous restaurant. Staying in family-run lodgings is a sure way to share local experiences, whether a farm with agritourism rooms or an elegant old villa where the owner chats with you over a *grappa* after dinner.

Above all, Italians are marked by their heartfelt hospitality and openness. Despite the many centuries that tourists have dutifully trudged upon a town's ancient stones, the Italians will still greet you cheerfully, help you find your way, suggest a favourite place to eat, try to understand your fractured attempts at pronunciation, and be genuinely glad to meet you.

Land and People

The borders separating Italy from its northern neighbours are tangible. The Alps and Dolomites form a solid wall, often a series of walls, so that access is over mountain passes or, more recently, through highway tunnels. Historically, such borders were easier to define and defend since they formed a natural barrier which discouraged random mingling.

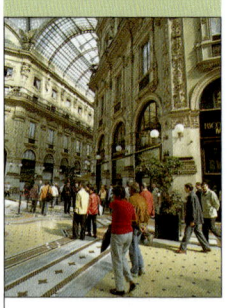

Galleria Vittorio Emanuele is Milan's favourite gathering-place

The same earth-changing forces that shaped these mountains gouged out the lakes that reflect them so prettily. Once the buckling and upheaving of the earth's crust thrust the Alps skywards, glaciers set to grinding them down. It was the glaciers that dug the fjord-like lakes, dropping the debris to form the hills that rise between the lakes and the flat valley of the Po River.

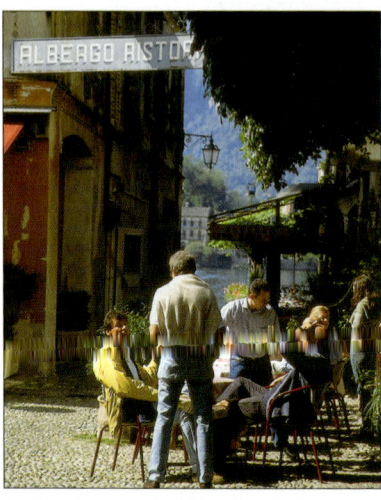

Sunday afternoons find lakeside cafés busy

The largest of the lakes are Maggiore, Como, Lugano, Iseo and Garda. South of these, a flat plain stretches from west of Milan to beyond Verona, continuing south to include the Po Valley.

Although the mountains form a wall to the north, the wall is not an even one. Each ridge or chain of peaks is cut and furrowed into a series of long ribs, separated by deep ravines that have been worn by meltwaters from the glaciers. As a result, the Alps lie like a crumpled newspaper. Hidden deep in these valleys are tiny communities, many of which have only recently become accessible by road. Their way of life contrasts sharply with that of the factory worker or banker in Milan – even though only a few dozen kilometres separate them.

Land shapes the people who live in the Lakes Region in two ways. It governs how they live, since they must choose occupations suited to it and lifestyles which enable them to survive there. Moreover, it governs who will stay and who will move on. Whatever the reason, the people who settled and remained in Italy's Alpine and sub-Alpine regions are an independent lot, self-sufficient and hard-working. The northern way of looking at life, in contrast to the come-what-may attitude of southern Italy, has shaped Milan and Lombardy since its earliest days as Roman Mediolanum. This outlook makes the wheels of Italian industry hum, and keeps its economy working.

History has shaped these northern Italians as well, since it was through here that all the migrations and conquering armies passed – or ebbed and flowed. The population, one could argue, is less 'Italian' and more mixed with Celtic, Lombard, Germanic and other peoples.

However, you will see less visible ethnic diversity in Northern Italy than elsewhere in Europe. Not that there isn't plenty of diversity among the Italians themselves, but there are fewer (although rising numbers) of Muslims, Asians and Blacks. Ethnic diversity lies more in the ways of life between the mountains and the plain, and in the influences of the language and culture of the neighbouring countries. Enter the Val d'Aosta and you will see the architecture change from stucco to stone and timber, and hear the accents change until the language becomes a blend of Italian and French. Climb into the mountains of northern Lombardy or the Trentino and you are suddenly in a land of chalets.

Bardolino's wine festival is a good place to mingle with local people

background

History

The first known inhabitants of the northern lake region were prehistoric peoples who lived in caves of the Valpolicella, near Verona, and Valcamonica, near Lake Iseo. Later, the Lugurians inhabited the Po Valley, but were overrun by the Celts in the 5th and 4th centuries BC.

The Visconti family ruled Milan in the 13th century

280 BC	Roman legions arrive in the Po Valley.
222 BC	Romans take Mediolanum (Milan).
218–200 BC	Second Punic War, Celts push Romans south of Po. Romans regain Mediolanum.
89 BC	People of Verona and Brescia gain full Roman citizenship.
15 BC	Mediolanum is made the capital of the Roman 11th region.
AD 313	Edict of Milan. Constantine recognises Christianity.
410	Visigoths invade from the north.
493–552	Ostrogoths under Theodoric seize control. Attila the Hun sacks Milan.
568–71	Lombards conquer northern region, and are converted to Christianity.
774	Charlemagne defeats Lombards, and is made King of the Lombards.
1155	Frederick Barbarossa is crowned Emperor of Holy Roman Empire.
1162	Barbarossa lays siege to Milan.

Fragments of Roman sculpture incorporated into Milan's Porta Nuova

1277	Visconti rule of Milan begins.
1559	Spain gains control over Milan region.
1560	Carlo Borromeo becomes the Bishop of Milan.
1706	Austrians occupy Milan.
1796	Milan occupied by the French under Napoleon.
1805	Napoleon is crowned King of Italy.
1814	Austria regains Lombardy.
1831	Giuseppe Mazzini founds Young Italy movement, beginning the resistance to Austria.
1848	First War of Italian Independence against Austrian rule, and the Papal State fails.
1858	Second War of Italian Independence. Battle of Solferino leads to founding of Red Cross.
1861	Vittorio Emanuele I is crowned King of Italy.
1870	Unification of the Kingdom of Italy is completed.
1915	Italy joins allies in the World War I against Germany.
1937	Hitler and Mussolini form pact, the Axis.
1940	Italy joins World War II as German ally.
1943	Mussolini deposed, sets up puppet state at Salo on Lake Garda.
1944	Italy joins allies; Italian partisans battle Nazis in occupied areas. Nazis blow up all the bridges in Verona.
1946	Vittorio Emanuele II abdicates. Republic of Italy declared.
1957	Italy joins European Economic Community, forerunner of European Union (EU).
1965	Milan's Duomo completed.
1970–85	Red Brigades terrorise Milan and other power centres.
1990s	Kickback scandals rock Milan's economic and political world.
2002	Italy adopts the euro.

background

Governance

If you are travelling to a country, it is good to know a little about how it is governed. Italy is a Parliamentary Republic, under a constitution adopted in 1948. It has a president and two legislative houses. The country is divided into 20 regions, whose governments have administrative powers, and those regions are further broken down into 94 provinces.

Italy's flag

This book covers most of the region of Lombardy, with parts of Piedmont, Valle d'Aosta, and the Veneto, and a small corner of the Trentino-Alto Adige. The top portion of Lago Maggiore and the central section of Lago Lugano lie in Switzerland, and are included as well.

While political boundaries within a country usually do not matter much to leisure travellers, it is handy to know that most tourism matters are administered by region. For example, a directory listing agri-tourism establishments will probably include only those in Lombardy or the Veneto, and so it helps to know what region you are in.

To further complicate the traveller's life, each province and each city has its own tourism brochures, tour maps and even offices. If the office belongs to the town (often called *pro loco*), they may have little information about their neighbours.

The larger lakes – Maggiore and Garda – are the dividing lines for regions, and so a trip around the lake will mean shifting from one set of tourist information to another and back again before the day is finished.

One thing you may notice while travelling in Italy is the strong sense of regional identity. Perhaps this stems from the fact that until it was unified in the 1870s, Italy was a series of small independent cities and states. It also reflects genuine differences in the regions – the Milanese has very little in common with the Sicilian.

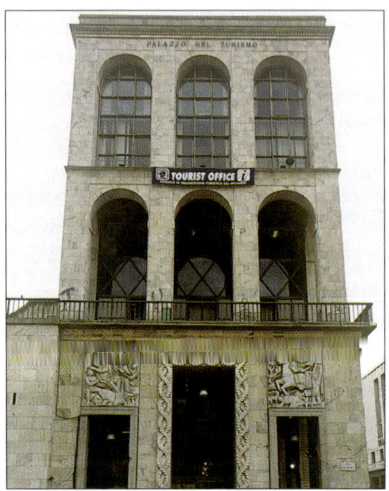
Department of Tourism building

background

Milan's elegant court building opposite Piazza Mercante

Rome in Northern Italy

As early as the 3rd century BC, the Romans had pushed their northern borders across the Po Valley and founded Mediolanum. The heart of this settlement – its forum – is now Milan's Piazza San Sepolcro, behind the Ambrosiana Museum. Punic Wars pushed the boundaries this way and that, but by the early 1st century AD, the Romans were secure enough to make Mediolanum the capital of their newest region.

By then other cities had begun to flourish. In the 1st century BC, residents of Brixia (Brescia) gained Roman citizenship. Augusta Pretoria (Aosta), on the Roman road to Gaul, grew from a legion way station to a city so thriving that it was known as the Rome of the Alps.

By the late 1st century AD, Verona already had a population large enough to build an arena seating more than 20,000 people. A grand villa was built on the point of Sirmeone on Lake Garda, and Romans colonised Lake Como's shores.

Not much of the Roman existence is visible in Milan. Some carved stone pieces have been incorporated into Porta Nuova, and the only remaining segment of the Roman wall is visible in the courtyard of the Civico Museo Archeologico (see p30).

Evidence of the Romans has fared better elsewhere. Aosta has much of its Roman theatre only because the standing wall was incorporated into other buildings, thus sealing and supporting it. Stripped of its covering for at least half a century, the theatre is again covered, this time in scaffolding which may remain for some years while structural repairs are made to save it. The stage, entrance and seating areas fill a large area before the standing wall, all

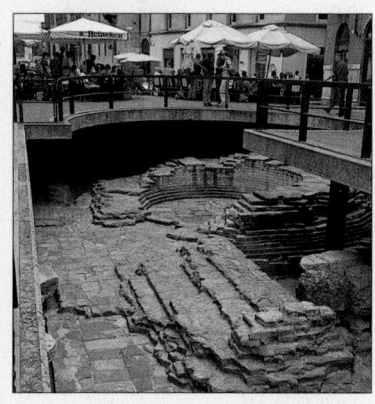

excavated. A Roman bridge and the impressive Arch of Augustus, built in 25 BC, remain, as do other arches, gates and portions of the original walls (see p51).

Elsewhere in the Val d'Aosta are Roman bridges at St Martin and St Vincent and an aqueduct at Pondel, as well as an arch over a section of Roman road at Donnas.

Verona preserves its arena, one of the three finest remaining, and the theatre overlooking a Roman bridge which was reconstructed after the World War II damage. Portions of the forum have been exposed under the pavement near Piazza Erbe, and an entire Roman gate, hidden for centuries in the wall of a building, has been revealed. Corsa Porta Borsari, Roman Verona's high street, still passes through the 1st-century gate of Porta Borsari. Another 1st-century Roman gate, Arco di Gavi, stands nearby, moved here along with the stone pavement that was beneath it, complete with chariot tracks (see pp140–41).

Brescia's forum, amphitheatre and Capitolium Temple have been uncovered and partially restored. Although there is more of the restoration than original in the Capitolium, it is clear what is original and the reconstruction gives a good picture of how the structures looked – far better than a row of fragments would. Other Roman treasures in Brescia, including an exquisite mosaic floor, are in the Civico Museo (see pp106–7).

No one knows exactly how much more of ancient Rome lies buried under pavements and grass or sealed inside buildings, but each new construction project turns up more pieces in the historic jigsaw puzzle.

Opposite: The excavated ruins of a Roman theatre in Aosta
Above: Verona's ancient Roman Forum
Below: Arco di Gavi, in Verona

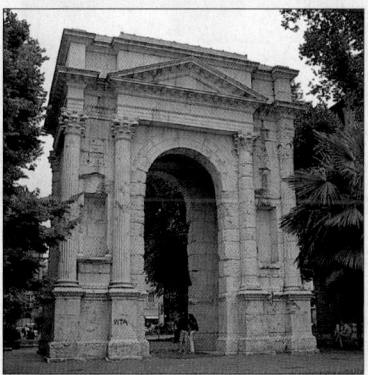

background

Culture

Think of the great names in the arts that are associated with Milan, Lombardy and the surrounding regions. Verdi, Donizetti and Toscanini in music; DaVinci and Bramante – artist and architect of the Renaissance; and the two great schools of architecture in the Middle Ages, the *maestri comacini* and the *maestro campionese*. And less familiar outside of Italy only because of the language difference, Manzoni and d'Annunzio in literature.

Cowbells from the Val d'Aosta

Consider the great arts venues of both La Scala – dream stage for every opera singer – and Verona's arena, home to one of Europe's three greatest opera festivals. Add to that the great clothing designers that have made Milan centre stage in fashion.

Wherever you travel in Milan and throughout the Lakes Region, you will find posters for concerts, many of which are free. These are held in churches (often with extraordinary acoustics), parks, palaces, *piazze* (squares) and even at the lakeside, and may feature a local quintet, a visiting choir or a fully-fledged concert orchestra. Tourist offices will usually have fliers or listings.

As important as the 'high' culture of the arts and design world is the popular culture that reaches into the soul of every Italian. Here traditions go deep, and local festivals still celebrate triumphs and deliverances from half a millennium ago. The simple rhythms of life and seasons are celebrated in festivals for just about every crop that is grown here, from cherries to wine.

Deep in a valley of the Gran Paradiso each September, farmers bring their best cows to the Battle of the Queens where the winners are awarded coveted decorated bells. In Mantova in May,

Lace-making is a fine art in Val d'Aosta

background

Spring and autumn are the best times to find these festivals, and reading local posters will point you in the right direction. Most are on at weekends, so watch for signs during the week and choose one to join. Local tourist offices can suggest others, and often publish a listing of events. One tip: the smaller the village and the more local the celebration, the more fun you will have and the more likely it is that you will soon become an 'insider' and join in.

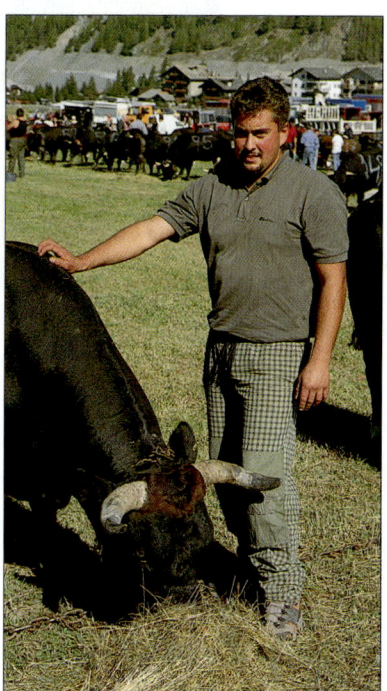

A farmer with his entry in the Battle of the Queens

a Medieval wedding is remembered with a costumed parade and flag-throwing, while local food producers give out samples of farm sausages and traditional cakes.

Each city, town and village has its saint day to observe with statues on parade, the local harvest to be thankful for, and local heroes to remember. It is not like the Italians to do these things quietly or without a party. Tents and temporary bandstands and dance floors will be thrown up in the square, food will be sold or given away, bands will play, and people will wear costumes.

A beekeeper displays his honey in Lazisi

background

Festivals and Events

From the world-renowned opera festival in Verona's Roman arena to the smallest local celebration of the harvest, Italians love an excuse to gather for music, food, wine, shopping and a good time. For the traveller, these are good opportunities to join local people and become a part of their world.

Posters announce local festivals

January
Mezzanotte Di Fabia, *Riva del Garda*
(New Year's Eve, fireworks)
Natale Nel Garda Trentino, *Garda Trentino*
(Concerts, entertainment and handicrafts)
Wise Men Processional, *Milano*

February
Carnevale di Verona, *Verona*
LP record fair at Parco di Esposizione, *Segrate*
Milan Carnevale, *Milano*

March
Gran Carnevale Di Arco, *Arco*
(Continues into March)
Oggi Aperto, *Milano*
(Milan Palazzi open house)
Trofeo Città di Arco, *Arco*
(International Youth Soccer tournament, continues into March)

April
Liberation Day, *throughout the region*
Liberation Festival, *Peschiera*
Palio del Recioto, *Negrar*
Stramilano, *Milano*
(In-town race, streets are closed)

May
Antica Fiera dei Mangiari
(Local produce, medieval dress, flag-throwing)
Concert, Sports at Idroscalo Park, *Linate*
(May through September)
Cortili Aperti, *Milano*
(Private courtyard open house)
Festa Del Caroccio, *Legnano*
(Parade commemorating 1176 battle, costumes)
Medieval White Wine Festival, *Soave*
Pittori Sul Naviglio, *Milano*
(Art exhibit along the Naviglio River)
Short Formats Festival, *Milano*
(Pan-European contemporary dance)
Square of Flavours, *Verona*
(Three-day festival of local produce and wines)

June
Festa del Naviglio, *Milano*
(Concerts, art, sports, cooking, antique market)
Festival of San Giovanni, *Isola Comacina*
(Fireworks)
Garda-Trentino Jazz Festival, *Riva del Garda*

Giro Italia, *Milano*
(Bike race finals)
Milano d'estate, *Milano*
(Concerts in Parco Sempione,
June–August)
Opera, *Arena di Verona*
(Performances through to August)
Sagra di San Cristororo, *Milano*
(Feast of the patron saint of drivers)
St Peter's Day, *Limone sul Garda*
(Fair, celebrations, fireworks)

July
Drodesera – *Centrale di Fies, Dro*
(Festival of avant-garde dance and
theatre, into August)
Fireworks Spectacular, *Sesto Calende*
Notturni in Villa, *Milano*
(Concerts in city villas)
Verona Vinorum, *Verona*
(Wine festival)

August
Ferragosto, *throughout the region*
(Feast of the Assumption, public holiday,
various celebrations)
Festival Del Film Di Locarno, *Locarno*
(Open-air screening in Piazza Grande,
ten days)
Honey and Apiary Festival, *Bosco*
Chiesanuova
Rustico Medioevo, *Canale di Tenno*
(Riva del Garda)
(Medieval dance and folklore)

September
Battaglia da Reina, *Cogne, Valle d'Aosta*
(Cattle show after their return from
summer pasture)
Festival Milano OLTRE90, *Milano*
(Festival of contemporary music, dance,
theatre, new media, continues through Oct)

Grape Festival, *Soave*
Italian Formula One Grand Prix,
Monza
(Grand Prix race, Parco di Monza)

October
Bardolino Wine Festival, *Bardolino*
Chestnut Festival, *San Mauro di Saline*
Festival Milano OLTRE90, *Milano*
(Festival of contemporary music, dance,
theatre, new media)
Honey Festival, *Lassizi*
Italian Fashion Design Show, *Milano*
(Not open to the public, but a host of
other activities occur)
Luoghi e Sapori in Terra Bresciana
(Festival of local food and wines)
Maratona di Verona, *Verona*
(Marathon race)
Marble Exposition, *Verona*
Milano International Film Festival,
Milano

November
Ancient Snail Fair, *Sant'Andrea-Badia*
Calavena
(Snail market, exhibition, truffles, food,
and crafts)
Tutti Santi, *throughout the region*
(All Saints' Day, public holiday)

December
Feast of Sant'Ambrogio, *Throughout the*
region
(7 December, public holiday)
Festa del Immacolata, *Throughout the*
region
(8 December, public holiday)
Milano Marathon, *Milano*
Stalls of Santa Lucia, *Verona*
(Christmas fair in Piazza Bra)

first steps

Impressions

Milan is a large, sprawling and often confusing city, and not one that visitors tend to fall in love with at first sight. However, it is well worth seeing and getting to know. The largest city in northern Italy, Milan is also the most culturally exciting, and a mecca for shoppers.

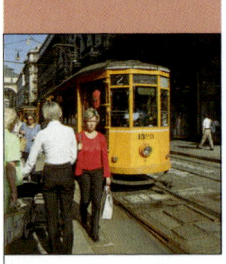

Old-fashioned streetcars lend colour to Milan's streets

Arriving in Milan
Northern Italy's major international airport is Malpensa, north of Milan, although many flights from within Europe arrive at Milan's smaller (and closer) Linate.

From the airport
Malpensa is roughly halfway between Milan and Lake Maggiore. Travellers bound for Como or Maggiore can go directly from the airport via express buses or by train from Milan's Centrale railway station. Express buses also connect to Milan's Centrale every 30 minutes from Malpensa, and every 20 minutes from Linate. This is the most convenient and least expensive way to get to Milan, although not necessarily the fastest.

WARNING

As in any airport, it is important to keep hold of your luggage at all times in Malpensa. More of a problem, however, is protecting your luggage when it emerges from under the bus in Milan. The best precaution is to be among the first off the bus, waiting for your bag when it appears.

Car hire
Major international rental companies are represented at Malpensa for pick up and delivery. All car rental firms are in Terminal 1. Most companies require a credit card, even if the hire has been prepaid. Before leaving the car park, make sure that you have all the registration and insurance documents, and that you know how to operate the vehicle. Don't plan a long day's driving after a long flight, especially if you are driving on the wrong side of the road.

If you are leasing a car from Renault (*see p180*), you can arrange to have it delivered to you at Malpensa for an extra charge. It is worth paying to avoid having to drive in Milan, particularly upon arrival.

Right-hand drive
The most immediate driving problem is the right-hand driving for those from left-hand drive countries, such as the UK and South Africa. In normal traffic, it soon begins to seem natural as you follow other drivers. But at roundabouts or on dual-lane highways, it becomes more difficult because your natural instincts give you the wrong signals. Be especially alert and continue to remind

first steps

Milan's Stazione Centrale, the central rail station

yourself of this danger. Ask a passenger to keep watch and remind you, at least until it becomes customary.

Entering Milan

In order to cut down on the amount of traffic in the city, a system of zones has been introduced. The city is divided into wedge-shaped areas within the ring road, and while you can enter and exit any sector from the ring road, you must leave that section and go around the ring road in order to enter another section. Thus, it is important to know where you are going before you enter the city.

Reserved lanes

In Milan, and occasionally elsewhere, there may be a lane reserved for buses, trams and taxis only. These are marked on the pavement, but are sometimes hard to see at night or if cars are close together in traffic.

Parking

Many car parks have coin-operated ticket dispensers. These are quite simple to use, even without being able to read the Italian instructions. In some places, tickets are at nearby news-stands. Put the ticket inside the windscreen so that it is visible from the outside. Some car parks are free, but have a limited stay of an hour or two. You can buy a paper 'clock' at news-stands, or write the time you arrive on a piece of paper.

Parking garages usually have a cashier on site. Take a time-stamped ticket when you enter and keep it with you. Before leaving, pay for the ticket at the *cassa* (cashier window), drive your vehicle to the exit and then insert the ticket to open the gate.

first steps

first steps

21

Travelling by Boat and Train

It is particularly appealing to explore the lakes by boat. Not only can you enjoy the best views of shore towns from the water, but the most convenient approach is by boat since most attractions are near the docks. And embarking on a boat, even a mundane car ferry, gives a trip the air of adventure.

Two basic kinds of boat ply the lakes: hydrofoils (*aliscafi*) and traditional lake 'steamers', which no longer operate on steam but retain the name. Hydrofoils are fast and especially good for long-distance trips, but they are not ideal for those who want to take photographs from the deck or enjoy leisurely views of lake scenery.

Rail connections in Italy are frequent, convenient and punctual. Milan is a hub

for several main railway lines and a number of smaller lines, including one that shuttles between Milan's Stazione Nord and Como's Milano Nord station, which is right at the boat docks. Train times on this line are designed to coincide with the boat schedule.

Stresa and Ancona (on Lake Maggiore), Lugano and Como are on major international railway lines between Switzerland and Milan. Garda is on the main Milan–Venice line and can be reached by a single connection off the rail route from Innsbruck, Austria.

Train stations are either a short walk from the boat landings or can be reached by frequent local buses or taxi, making it easy to travel to a base anywhere on the major lakes without a car. Once on the lake, boats connect to all other lake towns.

For information and schedules, contact: Navigazione Lago di Como, Piazza Cavour. Tel: (031) 579 211. www.navigazionelaghi.it. Navigazione del Lago di Lugano. Tel: (091) 923 1779.

www.lakelugano.ch. Navigazione Lago Maggiore. Tel: (800) 551 801. *www.navigazionelaghi.it.* Navigazione Lago di Garda. Tel: (030) 914 9511. *www.navigazionelaghi.it*

Money-saving passes

Holders of non-European passports can buy a variety of Eurail passes that make train travel more economical and easier. Many of these offer the flexibility of multi-day use over a period of a week or two (*www.eurail.com*). Likewise, each lake's navigation company offers a pass that allows one day's or several days' boat use for a fixed price. In each case, it is wise to consider your intended routes and decide if the pass will be cheaper than individual tickets.

Mountain tramways

Providing a different perspective on the lakes, several mountain tramways can lift you from lake towns to a bird's eye level and Alpine views. An aerial cable car (*funivia*) carries passengers from Stresa's Lido boat dock (Lake Maggiore) to the summit of Monte Mottarone, stopping at scenic Alpine gardens on the way (see pp56–7). From Malcesine, on Lake Garda, a new rotating *funivia* climbs Monte Baldo for views and another alpine garden (see pp118–19).

A venerable tram car (*funiculare*) leaves Como, close to the Milano Nord railway station and the boat landing, to reach the panoramic mountain village of Brunate (see p82). On Lake Lugano, a similar two-stage *funiculare* climbs Monte San Salvador from Paradiso, which can be reached by both boat and train (see p71).

Opposite above: Water taxis provide fast service between lake towns
Opposite below: Funicular lines climb lake-side mountains for sweeping views
Above: Excursion boats provide scenic tours and access to lake towns

what to see

Milan

Smart, busy, self-confident, prosperous and a little bit cocky, Milan is the unofficial capital of Italy. The government may be in Rome, but the strings are pulled from here. At least the purse strings are, for Milan is the country's commercial and economic epicentre. And, in the high-wire world of fashion, Milan is the capital of all Europe. All but Parisians (and even some of them) look to Milan's catwalks to see it first.

Milan's Duomo is topped by delicate pinnacles

While Milan is the arrival point for most travellers to Northern Italy, and the goal of business people attending the many major trade shows at the Fiera di Milano, it is not a major destination for tourists. Most swing through to see *The Last Supper* and the Duomo, or to shop, but tend to ignore its many other attractions.

what to see

Although the city sprawls over an increasing area of the Po plain, most of its historical and artistic sights are within a reasonable walk from the Duomo, which is – and should be – everyone's first stop. Even the fashion houses of the *Quadrilatero della Moda* (Fashion Quarter) are only a few blocks from the cathedral's stony frills and leering gargoyles.

Within 2.59sq km (a square mile) are eye-boggling art collections, the world's most famous opera house, historic churches which are art museums in their own right, smart shops, and a Renaissance castle. Da Vinci, Caruso, Verdi, Armani and a chapelful of saints have all worked in this golden mile. St Augustine was baptised under what is now the pavement of Piazza della Duomo, Napoleon was crowned inside the church, Toscanini conducted at La Scala, and Verdi died just around the corner. It is no wonder that Milan has a bit of a superiority complex.

Driving in Milan is not for the faint of heart

Castello Sforzesco

Connected to Piazza Duomo by the wide Via Dante, Castello Sforzesco makes an elegant home for a group of city museums. Its construction and embellishment spanned a century from the 1360s to the 1450s, with some creative reconstruction at the turn of the 20th century. The dukes hired the very best to work here, including Bramante and Leonardo da Vinci.

When the Spanish had control of Milan in the 16th and 17th centuries, they built fortifications around the outside of the castle walls. By the time Napoleon came to town, the walls had deteriorated badly and he ordered them to be torn down immediately.

If the museums are closed, a walk through the castle is still worthwhile since a number of its attractions are visible. Inside the loggia of the **Corte Ducale** are frescoes and in the Cortile della Rocchetta, opposite, is a glass-housed display of architectural and ornamental stone carving.

In Piazza Castello an impressive fountain can be found, fondly dubbed the *tort de' spus* (wedding cake) by the Milanese.

Museo d'Arte Antica

Particularly outstanding are the collections of sculpture from the Middle Ages and Renaissance. Michelangelo's last work, the *Pieta Rondanini*, in progress when he died, is the attention-getter. However, the Busti tomb sculptures are also Renaissance masterpieces. Many of the works here were saved from churches and convents that were being demolished. *Tel. (02) 8846 3731.*

Museo d'Arte Antica Armeria

Weaponry and armour collections are arranged to show how armour changed to match the technology of weaponry.

The rooms of this section are joined by magnificent carved marble arches. *Tel: (02) 8846 3660.*

Museo delle Arti Decorative

Filling galleries off two courtyards, this wide-ranging museum has displays of clocks, ironwork, ceramics, wooden sculpture, ivory, jewellery and Italy's largest collection of furniture. The 12 Trivulzio tapestries are considered the foremost masterpieces of Renaissance textiles. The origins of Milan's pre-eminence in fashion are explored in a collection of costumes, beginning with the 17th century.

Musei dei Castello Sforzesco, Pza Castello. Open: Tue–Sun 9am–5.30pm. Castle grounds open daily 8am–8pm. Free admission. Metro: Cadorna or Cairoli. The castle is undergoing major restoration, so portions are closed from time to time. The tourist office has a brochure, 'MilanoMusei', detailing the updated status.

Museo degli Strumenti Musicali

From pocket-sized violins and Medieval lutes to hurdy-gurdies, this museum combines the technology of sound with the artistry of creating fine wood and metal crafts. A rare 1520 instrument is one of the earliest surviving.

Museo della Preistoria e Protostoria

Paleolithic, Neolithic and Iron Age artefacts, especially those from the Po Valley, are the focus.
Tel: (02) 8846 3702.

Pinoteca

Paintings from Medieval times through to the 18th century include works of Mantegna, Lotto, Bellini and Canaletto. The 20th-century art collection, one of Europe's best, features Picasso and his contemporaries. *Tel: (02) 8846 3731.*

Opposite: The 'wedding cake' fountain
Above: Medieval house façades in the castle walls

what to see

Walk: The Duomo

The first Duke of Milan commissioned Italy's grandest gothic cathedral before his death in 1402, stirred into action at the prodding of the Archbishop. The third largest Christian church in the world and the artistic apex of the flamboyant gothic, Milan's Duomo is almost encrusted with statuary – more than 2,000 statues stand in niches or atop pinnacles on the exterior alone. Dozens of delicately carved spires laden with stone curlicues reach skyward from its roof, and stand out in relief above the heads of statues.

Open daily: 7am–6.45pm. Metro: Duomo.
Allow 1 hour.

1 Entrance
The bronze panels covering the central doors, although started in the mid-1800s, were not completed until 1966. Inside, the 52 soaring columns of the nave and aisles draw your eyes upward to the vaulted ceiling.
Turn right to the kiosk for tickets, returning to the passageway beside the central door.

2 Paleochristian Baptistery
Excavations beneath the piazza disclose the circular **Baptistery of San Giovani alle Fonti**, where St Ambrose baptised St Augustine in AD 387. Some mosaics and patterned marble floor remain and glass cases show stone carving and other artefacts discovered here and in the adjoining **Basilica de San Tecla** excavations.
Return to the nave and turn right to the south aisle.

3 Bishop d'Intimiano Sarcophagus
In the first of the elaborately corniced side altars, the sarcophagus is a fine example of 11th-century stone work. Note the 15th- and 16th-century stained glass windows in the first chapels along this aisle, the cathedral's oldest.

4 Medici tomb

In the south transept is the tomb of Gian Giacamo de'Medici, by the 16th-century sculptor Leone Leoni. His muse was clearly Michelangelo. The transept, or crossing, where two grand altars face each other, is a good place to admire the rows of statues which sit on top of the nave's columns.

Continue around the outer wall, past the startlingly realistic St Bartholomew, into the semi-circular ambulatory.

5 Crypt

Below the high altar is the tomb of San Carlo Borromeo (*see p56*). If the crypt is not open, there are good views into it from the ambulatory.

6 Ambulatory windows

The brilliant stained glass windows enclosing the apse are the work of the brothers Bertini, crafted in the 19th century. Representing biblical scenes, the windows are some of the finest examples of the refinement that the art had reached.

Continue around to the steps ascending to the high altar.

7 Choir

Behind the high altar, the choir (*Open: Mon–Fri 1.30–5pm, Sat 1.30–4pm*) is surrounded by richly carved panels in deep relief. Under the seats, misericords are carved as lion and angel heads.

Return to the ambulatory and continue into the transept.

8 Trivulzio Candelabrum

In the north transept, the 12th-century candelabrum depicts fantastic creatures,

Bronze panels decorate the Duomo's central doors

the masterpiece of goldsmith Nicholas of Verdun. Note the pair of copper pulpits that flanks the high altar.

Continue along the aisle towards the entrance.

9 Cappella del Crocifisso

Off the north aisle, and reserved for prayer, is a chapel honouring the crucifix that was carried by San Carlo Borromeo in a 1576 procession praying for deliverance from the plague. The stained glass is 16th century.

Cross the transept, exiting the north side and turn left.

10 La Salita (roof)

A lift (or stairway) ascends to the roof top, one of Milan's highlights. Here you can wander among the delicate spires and statues and, on clear days, get a breathtaking view of the Alps.

what to see

Casa del Manzoni

Although not well known outside of the country, Manzoni's work, *I Promessi Sposi* (*The Betrothed*), is on the reading list in every Italian school, right up there with Dante. Playing on the theme of love thwarted, Manzoni brought immediacy to his 19th-century Italian readers by weaving in both political and religious themes and characters, conflicts that ring true even today.

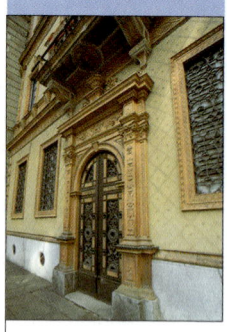

The facade of Casa del Manzoni

Behind the highly decorative facade of his eclectic-style home, where he lived from its completion in 1864 until his death (by falling down the steps of neighbouring San Fedele) in 1873, all is just as he left it, including the study where he wrote much of his work.
Via Morone 1. Tel: (02) 8646 0403. Open: Tue–Fri 9am–noon & 2–6pm. Free admission. Metro: Duomo.

CIMAC
Known by its acronym, the Civico Museo di Arte Contemporanea, is on the upper floor of **Palazzo Reale**, which faces the south side of the Duomo, beside the tourist office. Built as the palace of the Archduke of Austria in the late 1700s when Milan was under Hapsburg rule, the palace's regal interior was adorned with frescoes and stucco work, much of which was destroyed in World War II. Along with the city's permanent collections of 20th-century art, the palace houses the small **Museo del Duomo**. Major travelling or temporary art exhibits are shown here, usually advertised by banners on the facade.
Piazza del Duomo. Tel: (02) 3932 2737. Hours vary with current exhibit. Metro: Duomo.

Cimitero Monumentale
Monumental is the key word in this astonishing final resting place of the once rich and famous. Art Nouveau – called Liberty style here – is at its height in the earlier tombs and monuments, which date from the late 1800s to the mid-20th century. A map, in English, leads to some highlights. The inner circle – Milan's *illuminati* – are buried within the Famae Aedes, and include conductor Arturo Toscanini, poet Salvatore Quasimodo and author Alessandro Manzoni (*see Casa del Manzoni, above*). Many of the monuments are by noted Italian sculptors.
Four blocks north of Stazione Porta Garibaldi. Tel: (02) 659 9938. Open: Tue–Fri 8.30am–5.15pm, Sat–Sun 8.30am–5.45pm. Free admission. Tram: 3, 4.

Civico Museo Archeologico
Opposite the high baroque Palazzo Arese Litta, the convent of the church of

what to see

San Maurizio now houses the city's archaeological collections, the highlights of which relate to Roman Milan. The location was not chosen at random for it sits over portions of the original Roman walls, visible beneath the courtyard, along with a 24-sided Roman tower, **Torre Ansperto**. A model shows what Roman Mediolanum, the original Milan, looked like. The museum also features Greek and Etruscan art and terracotta pieces and ancient Greek ivories from Appulia. It is worth stepping into **San Maurizio** itself (*Open: Tue–Sun 9am–noon & 2–5.30pm*) to see the excellent frescoes by Bernardo Luini and his sons. These almost completely cover the interior, their colours still vibrant after half a millennium.
Corso Magenta 15. Tel: (02) 8645 0011. Open: Tue–Sun 9.30am–5.30pm. Free admission. Metro: Cadorna.

Entrance to the archaeology museum at San Maurizio

Milan's Architecture

Despite the loss of its buildings to modernisation and war, Milan's architecture covers almost 2,200 years – from Rome's conquest to today's monuments to the gods of commerce. Every major style is encapsulated, adapted and reshaped to reflect Milan's own culture.

Little of Roman Mediolanum remains (see pp12–13), but outside San Lorenzo Maggiore, which may have been part of the Roman imperial palace chapel, stand 16 Roman columns from the 2nd and 3rd centuries BC. In the centre is a statue that commemorates the AD 313 Edict of Milan, which ended the persecution of Christians.

The Edict of Milan proved to be a significant event in Lombard architecture, unleashing a flurry of church building. Roman forms were adapted to churches; San Lorenzo, built within decades of the Edict, also incorporates material from other Roman structures.

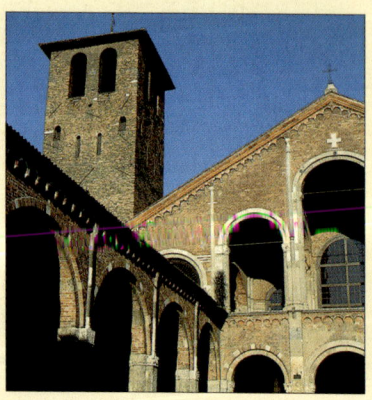

Sant'Ambrogio, AD 379–86, is another fine example of early Christian architecture. Its interior adapts the massive solidity of the Roman basilica – a long hall ending in an apse and flanked by two columned aisles. The portico and interior also reflect the 11th–12th-century Romanesque style popular in the early Middle Ages (see pp42–3).

This was when the Gothic form developed. New building techniques, especially flying buttresses, allowed for lighter, less massive walls and made large windows possible. Milan's Duomo (see pp28–9) is the best example of this exuberant style with its forest of spires and over 2,000 saints perched in their niches. The nave, begun in 1385, is pure northern Gothic, one of the few in Italy.

When the Sforza family took over Milan in 1450, they brought in two of the leading Renaissance architects – Antonio Averulino (Il Filarete) and

Donato Bramante – who were both greatly influenced by Roman ideals. One of Averulino's first projects was remaking Castello Sforzesco (see pp26–7), and the University of Milan is another Averulino building, its cruciform shape revolutionary and its mix of brick and terracotta brilliant.

Bramante, who began his work in Milan before going to Rome, showed his genius at Santa Maria Presso San Satiro (see p45), where the Renaissance facade gives way to a masterpiece of trompe l'oeil behind the altar.

As the Renaissance progressed into Mannerism, less attention was paid to classic orders, a trend that culminated in the Baroque where the straight lines yielded to the curve. In Milan this trend was led by Pelligrino Tibaldi, under the patronage of Cardinals Carlo and Federico Borromeo. The Jesuit church of San Fedele (see p42) is an example of his work.

Neo-classicism signalled a return to Roman and Greek forms, advocated in Milan by Giuseppe Piermarini. His Palazzo Reale, built next to the Duomo for the Hapsburgs during the Austrian occupation, was rebuilt after serious World War II damage. He also designed the Teatro alla Scala, similarly rebuilt after bombing.

Along with Austria, France occupied Milan before its unification, and the French Second Empire influence shows in the splendid glass-domed Galleria Vittorio Emanuele II (see p34). Shortly after, Camillo Boito designed Cimiterio Monumentale, whose eclectic style looked ahead to Art Nouveau. The city continued in this direction with the memorial monuments which are among Milan's finest examples of the style (see p31).

A 1902 decorative arts exposition prompted Italian designers to shape Art Nouveau into the uniquely Italian Liberty style. After World War I, European modernism pushed this into Novecento style, particularly favoured by Mussolini and the Fascists. Characterised by clean, flat facades broken by striking relief panels of modernist, stylised heroic figures, a good example is the tourist office building on Piazza del Duomo.

Opposite top: Galleria Vittorio Emanuele
Opposite bottom: The portico and tower of Sant' Ambrogio
Below: Novecento decorative panel

what to see

Galleria Vittorio Emanuele II
If any one image symbolises Milan, it is this elegantly turned-out shopping mall between Piazza del Duomo and Piazza de La Scala. Despite the price tags in its shops and cafés, the Milanese use its grand glass-domed arcades so much that they call it their 'living room'. Built in the middle of the 19th century, it was the largest shopping complex in Europe, and marked the beginning of modern architecture in Italy. Under its 48m (157ft) high dome, the *crème de la crème* of shops sell silverware, high fashion, jewellery and other, more mundane, items. But mostly it is about the cafés, from whose tables half of Milan watches the other half.
Pza del Duomo. Open: daily 24 hours. Shops open: Mon–Sat 9.30am–1pm & 3.30–7pm. Metro: Duomo.

Giardini Publici
Businesslike Milanese don't give up much pavement space for greenery, but when they do, they do it right. From Piazza Cavour to the line of the former city walls, spreads an oasis of lawns, wooded reaches, gardens, pools, fountains, winding paths, playgrounds, a café and a healthy collection of museums. Most of the garden was laid out as parkland in the 1780s and, in 1871, the whole lot, including adjacent villa grounds, was revamped for the World Expo. Inside the gardens are the small **Museo del Cinema** in Palazzo Dugnani (*Tel: (02) 655 4977. Open: Fri–Sun 3–6.30pm. Admission charge.*) **Civica Museo di Storio Naturale** (Natural History Museum) (*Tel: (02) 8846 3280. Open: Tue–Sun 9am–6pm. Free admission*), and the **Planetario Ulrico Hoepli** (*Tel: (02) 2953 1181. Open for planetarium shows*).

La Scala
Although it is unclear exactly when the great 1778 opera house will reopen after its structural renovation, it is certain that the theatre will look just as it did, its Carrara marble and elaborate chandeliers gleaming. Meanwhile – and this will be at least throughout 2004, possibly longer – performances are staged at Teatro Acimboldi (*see pp156–7*) and the theatre's museum has been installed in a small *palazzo* opposite the church of Santa Maria del Grazie (*see below*).
Pza della Scala. Tel: (02) 805 3418.

La Scala opened in 1778

what to see

Museo La Scala

Happily ensconced in temporary quarters during the reconstruction, the opera house's museum will fascinate lovers of opera and music. The setting, at least throughout 2004, is a gem of a *palazzo*, with excellent fresco and stucco work. The highlights of the museum's collections are so well exhibited here that one wonders if perhaps they might stay. Wherever the museum settles, it will contain costumes worn by the great divas – Leonine Price as Aida, Maria Callas as Anne Boleyn, Renata Tibaldi as Manon Lescault. Original designer sketches for costumes and stage sets, including the actual Birnam Wood from *Macbeth*, and the original deed for the theatre signed by King Vittorio Emanuele II join a touching display of the items on Verdi's desk at the time of his death. An automated ticket sales point makes it possible to purchase seats by credit card.

Palazzo Busca, Corso Magenta 71.
Tel: (02) 469 1249, www.teatroallascala.it
Open: daily 9am–6pm. Admission charge.
Metro: Cadorna.

Galleria Vittorio Emanuele was Italy's first major work of modern architecture

what to see

Museo Nazionale Scienza e della Tecnica Leonardo da Vinci

For those unable to understand the Italian explanations on the exhibits of Italy's notable scientific and technical achievements, the Leonardo da Vinci Gallery is the place to head. Displayed here are his drawings and documents with models, in easy-to-understand exhibits, which follow the great inventor's contributions to science. Maritime enthusiasts will not want to miss the collection of ship models in the **Museo Navale**. The museum surrounds the Renaissance cloister of the former convent of San Vittore al Corpo, whose adjacent church is one of the most highly decorated churches in the city, with works by several Renaissance artists of the Milanese school. The inlaid choir stalls are from the same period.
Via San Vittore 21. Tel: (02) 485 551. www.museoscienza.org. Open Tue–Fri 9.30am–4.30pm, Sat–Sun 9.30am–6.50pm. Admission charge. Metro: Sant'Ambrogio.

Museo Poldi Pezzoli

Far more than an art gallery, this private museum was founded by an avid 19th-century collector. Paintings are mixed with collections ranging from Lombard enamels to armour and textiles, all in the context of a furnished period house. Works by Boticelli, Mantegna, Bellini and Tiepolo mix with displays of Murano glass and Coptic fabrics. Brochures and free audio tours are available in English.
Via Manzoni 12. Tel: (02) 794 889. Open Tue–Sun 10am–6pm. Admission charge, reduced Wed. Metro: Montenapoleone.

The Poldi Pezzoli museum

Museo Zucchi

Perhaps the city's quirkiest museum, this one occupies the basement of a store just off Piazza Duomo. It displays thousands of hand-printing blocks, some dating from the 1700s, used for applying designs on fabric, a subject close to the heart of Milan's fashion industry. A short video shows the techniques used.
Via Ugo Foscolo 4. Tel: (02) 9025 5230. Open Mon 3.30–7pm, Tue–Sat 10.30am–7.30pm. Free admission. Metro: Duomo.

Palazzo Bagatti Valsecchi

A tour here is more akin to visiting the home of a highly cultured and wealthy family than a museum. The two courtyards of this *palazzo* face each other across a street in the middle of

what to see

the fashion district, both worth investigating, even if you don't stop to tour the museum. Although built in the late 1800s, the *palazzo* was intended to house collections from the 16th century and was designed according to Renaissance aesthetic notions. The emphasis of the museum is on the art of collecting, as well as on the objects themselves. These are nonetheless impressive, with tapestries, furniture (including children's), rare manuscripts, and paintings by the Renaissance masters. Information on the collections in each room is posted in English. If you would like to savour this house at more leisure, ask to have your ticket stamped for another visit.

Via San Spirito 10. Tel: (02) 7600 6132. Open: Tue–Sun 1–5.45pm. Closed: Aug. Admission charge, reduced Wed. Metro: Montenapoleone.

Palazzo Bagatti Valsecchi sits in the centre of the fashion district

Piazza Mercante

In a city with a history of overzealous urban renovation and wartime bombing, it is a pleasant surprise to find this Medieval enclave opposite the 16th-century law courts, just off Piazza Duomo. Built in 1233, the **Palazzo della Ragione** was originally the town hall, the political centre of Medieval Milan, and the open arcade beneath it was the market. The black and white marble Palazzo degli Osii, built in 1316, forms the other side, overlooking a now quiet square where booksellers often set up shop.

Pinacoteca Ambrosiana

Commissioned by Cardinal Frederico Borromeo to house the valuable collection of documents that it still contains Pinacoteca Ambrosiana was one of the world's first public libraries when it opened in 1609. The Cardinal's personal art collection was added in 1618, making this an exceptionally rich concentration of arts and letters. On exhibit are paintings by Leonardo da Vinci, Caravaggio and Brueghel, as well as Raphael's cartoons for his Vatican frescoes. Lord Byron is said to have stolen a strand of Lucretia Borgia's hair

An old well is in the centre of one of the Palazzo Bagatti Valsecchi's courtyards

from the museum in 1816. The original facade, facing Piazza San Sepolcro, is now the back of the museum.
Pza Pio XI 2. Tel: (02) 806 921. Open: Tue–Sat 10am–5.30pm. Admission charge. Metro: Duomo.

Pinacoteca Di Brera
Milan's largest art museum (not an inconsiderable title in this art-filled city) is a vast complex broken by courtyards. Both the best-known and the lesser-known Italian masters are represented, including Caravaggio, Piero della Francesca, Titian, Raphael, Tintoretto, Veronese, Luini, Bramante, Mantegna, Tiepolo and Canaletto. However, it is not only Italian Renaissance paintings; works of Rembrandt, Van Dyck, Braque, Picasso and Modigliani join them. Much of the largess was acquired when the monasteries were closed under Napoleon's rule. The streets surrounding the Pinacoteca are worth exploring for the small galleries, artists' studios and Left-Bank ambience of its cafés.
Via Brera 28. Tel: (02) 722 631. www.brera.beniculturali.it. Open: Tue–Sat 8.30am–7.30pm, Sun 9am–1pm.

Quadrilatero della Moda (Fashion Quarter)
Although the catwalks of Fiera di Milano are visible only to those with trade credentials, anyone can enjoy the spectacle of the season's most outrageous – and expensive – fashions simply by strolling along the streets where the designers have their shops. These cluster in the streets south of Piazza Cavour, off Via Monte Napoleone. Among the shop windows of designer boutiques are some lovely old homes and *palazzi*, whose inner courtyards are often visible. Before compromising your credit card in the shops, remember that Milanese rarely wear the flamboyant duds in the windows, and that doing so will mark you as a tourist wannabe.
Streets in the area bounded by Via Monte Napoleone, Via La Spiga, Via San Andrea and Via Manzoni. Metro: Monte Napoleone.

San Bernardino alle Ossa
This is perhaps one of Milan's most unsettling churches, where the walls of the Capella Ossario (Ossuary Chapel) are lined with human bones arranged in patterns. Although this is not an uncommon practice in Iberia, it is seen less often in Italian churches.
Pza San Stefano. Open: Mon–Fri 7.30am–noon & 2.30–6pm, Sat–Sun 7.30am–noon. Metro: Duomo.

Statue overlooking Piazza Mercante

Walk: Central Milan

While Milan sprawls for a considerable distance, many of its primary sights are relatively close to the Duomo. This route takes you past many of them.

Allow 2 hours, longer with Duomo and museum tours.

Begin at Piazza del Duomo, where the tourist information office can supply maps and current museum and church opening hours, which are good to consult since these change frequently.

1 The Duomo
You can't miss the elaborate exterior, unless it is enclosed in scaffolding (*see pp28–9*).
Leaving the Duomo, walk straight ahead from the left corner of the piazza onto Via Torino.

2 Santa Maria presso San Satiro
Among the windows on the left-hand side of this popular shopping street is a small opening, almost hidden by a flower vendor, leading to this surprising Bramante church (*see p45*).

The unusual facade of Casa degli Omenoni

Cross Via Torino and follow Via Spadari to Via Cantu, turning right. Cross Via Orefici.

3 Piazza Mercante
Opposite Via Cantu, go through the narrow passage into the centre of Medieval Milan (*see p38*). Beyond the arcade is Via Mercante, under the gaze of St Ambrose, whose statue adorns the old law courts.
Turn right and cross the street, entering the arcaded northern side of Piazza del Duomo.

4 Galleria Vittorio Emanuele II
To your left is the grand glass-domed gallery (*see p34*).
Walk through to the far end.

5 Piazza della Scala
Directly ahead as you exit the Galleria is La Scala, the world's best-known opera venue (*see p34*). To your right is Palazzo Marino, Milan's city hall.
Leave the piazza at the far side, along Via Case Rotte, circling Palazzo Marino to see its more attractive facade on Piazza San Fedele.

6 San Fedele
The Jesuit church is on the left (*see p42*).
Backtrack a few steps into Largo Raffaele

Mattioli and walk straight through to Via Omenoni.

7 Casa degli Omenoni
The street passes under the oversized statues on the facade of the house designed by the sculptor Leone Leoni in 1500.
At the end, turn left.

8 Casa del Manzoni
At the end of the square is the eclectic-style facade of the home of the writer, Manzoni (*see p30*).
Follow Via Gerolamo Morone beside the Manzoni house, to its end, turning right.

9 Via Alessandro Manzoni
One of Milan's most elegant streets, Via Manzoni is flanked by *palazzi*, whose archways lead into leafy courtyards. Several are open to explore.

10 Museo Poldi Pezzoli
On the right, behind an elegant facade, is this *palazzo*-turned-art-museum (*see p36*). Further on, across the street, is the Grand Hotel where the composer Guiseppi Verdi died.
Turn right at Via Monte Napoleone.

11 Quadrilatero della Moda
Wander the streets enclosed by Via Monte Napoleone, Via Della Spiga, Via San Andrea and Via Manzoni to see the window displays of the great fashion houses (*see p39*).

12 Palazzo Bagatti Valsecchi
One of these streets is Via San Spirito, which runs between the facing courtyards of this Renaissance-style *palazzo* (*see p37*).
Return to your starting point by Metro from Monte Napoleone.

what to see

San Fedele

The somewhat severe, highly disciplined Jesuit style is greatly enlivened by baroque flourishes, showing each at its best. San Fedele is one of Pellegrino Tibaldi's earliest works, and his skill in interpreting the new ideas of the Counter Reformation made him a favourite of Cardinal Borromeo, whose hand was in every project of mid-1500s' Milan. Baroque and Mannerist (late Renaissance) paintings abound, as does Baroque wood carving, especially on the confessionals. The carved choir stalls are not original to the church – they were moved here from Santa Maria della Scala when it was torn down to build the opera house.
Pza San Fedele. Tel: (02) 7200 8027. Open: daily 7.30am–2.30pm & 4–7pm. Metro: Duomo.

The interior of San Sebastiano

San Sebastiano

Five years after designing San Fedele, Tibaldi was chosen by Cardinal Borromeo to design this church in thanksgiving for Milan's deliverance from the plague. The Comerio painting inside the colossal dome is impressive, not so much for its artistic virtuosity as for its size. The round interior still glows with the flickering candles lit in votive offering before the various altars.
Via Torino. Tel: (02) 874 263. Open: Mon–Sat 8am–noon & 3–5pm, Sun 9.30am–12.30pm & 3.30–7pm. Metro: Duomo.

San Sepulcro

Dedicated to the Holy Sepulchre in Jerusalem, San Sepulcro sits in the heart of what was once the forum of Roman Milan, or Mediolanum. Reworked in the Counter Reformation under Cardinal Carlo Borromeo and again at the end of the 19th century, there is little left of the Romanesque church except for its long crypt, little changed since the church's construction in 1030. There is a sarcophagus from the 1500s in the apse, with good stone carvings.
Pza San Sepulcro. Open: Mon–Fri noon–2.30pm, Mass at 12.45pm. Metro: Duomo.

Sant'Ambrogio

The most historic of Milan's many remarkable churches, Sant'Ambrogio was started by Milan's own Sant'Ambrogio in the 4th century AD, and has led a far from quiet life: in 1196, the dome collapsed and was rebuilt, and in 1943 the church was badly damaged by bombing. Additions made in the interim – a monastery

Carved Romanesque capitals at Sant'Ambrogio

(8th century), two bell towers (9th and 12th centuries) the large portico (9th century) and a number of interior embellishments – have made the church a living museum. The atrium, which has excellent carved capitals on its columns, is one of Europe's most important examples of the Romanesque period. From it, a 4th-century portal with stone carvings and 9th-century bronze doors leads inside. Ahead, beneath an outstanding pulpit, is the **Stilicone sarcophagus**, here since the 4th century and surrounded with exceptional deep-relief carvings.

The golden altarpiece, inset with stones, was created by master goldsmiths in the time of Charlemagne (after AD 774), and under it is a crypt with the remains of not one, but three saints: Ambrose himself and the two Milanese martyrs for whom he built the church. Through the last chapel on the right is the vibrant mosaic dome of the original 4th-century **Sacello de San Vittore**.
Pza Sant'Ambrogio 15. Tel: (02) 8645 0895. Open: Mon–Sat 7am–noon & 2–7pm, Sun 7am–1.15pm & 2.30–7.45pm. Treasury: daily 9.30am–noon & 2.30–6pm. Metro: Sant'Ambrogio.

Sant'Eustorgio

The 11th-century church was rebuilt in the following century after being destroyed by Holy Roman Emperor, Frederick Barbarossa, in his siege of Milan. When Barbarossa left, he took with him the most sacred of the church's treasury – the relics of the Three Kings. These were returned much later, and are venerated on Epiphany (6 January). The church was rebuilt and renovated so often that it has a little bit of everything, from Romanesque forward, and a little bit of everybody in the local late Medieval art world, including Luini and Balduccio, whose marble tomb of Stephano Visconti is an outstanding example of high Gothic.

The church's place in art history, however, is assured by the **Cappella Portinari**, behind the apse – Milan's first real Renaissance ensemble. Commissioned in the 1460s by a Medici banker from Florence as a tomb for himself and St Peter Martyr (humility was never a strong Florentine suite), the chapel brings together the work of Balduccio (his reliquary arc is in the chapel's centre) and Foppa, whose frescoes here are considered his masterpiece. The Foppa fresco cycle shows scenes in the life of St Peter Martyr, with dancing angels around the base of the dome.

Pza Sant'Eustorgio. Tel: (02) 5810 1583. Church open: daily 7.45am–noon & 3.30–6.30pm. Chapel open: Tue–Sun 10am–6pm (July–Aug 4–6.30pm). Admission charge to chapel. Tram: No 3.

Santa Maria della Grazie

Bramante gave this 15th-century Gothic church its Renaissance appearance by rebuilding the sanctuary and apse and adding the charming 'Frog Cloister'. Inside, in the second chapel on the right, a Caravaggio painting stands in for the Titian stolen by Napoleon's army in 1797 and taken off to the Louvre, where it remains.

In the adjoining **Cenacolo Vinciano** is one of the most widely recognised of all paintings, Leonardo da Vinci's *The Last Supper*. Painted during 1496–7, on a dry surface that began to deteriorate almost immediately, the work captures the moment of shock and disbelief as Christ announces that one of his disciples will betray him. The work's power is intensified by the use of a stable base which allowed da Vinci more time to concentrate on details of facial expression, difficult in the volatile fresco

Bramante's altar at Santa Maria presso San Satiro

what to see

medium. Generally regarded as one of the great masterpieces of Western art, the painting shows the ravages of time despite recent restoration.
Pza Santa Maria delle Grazie.
Tel: (02) 8942 1146, from outside Italy +39 (02) 8942 1146. Church open: daily 7am–noon & 3–7pm, Cenacolo Tue–Sun 8.15am–6.45pm. Admission charge. Timed Cenacolo tickets must be reserved in advance; operators speak English. Metro: Conciliazione.

Santa Maria presso San Satiro

It is best to enter this church before reading about it, admiring the deep-vaulted sanctuary from the entrance before walking closer to realise that its depth is a very skilfully designed illusion. Lacking the space for a grand apse behind the altar, Bramante created, in less than a metre (3.28ft), the optical illusion of a sanctuary worthy of a cathedral. The Cappella della Pieta, to the left, has some early Medieval frescoes.
Via Torino 9. Tel: (02) 7202 1804.
Open: Mon–Sat 8.30–11.30am & 3.30–5.30pm, Sun 9.30–10.30am & 4.30–5.30pm. Metro: Duomo.

The church of Santa Maria della Grazie

Train and Boat Tour: Lake Como from Milan

Milan is so close to the town of Como, the gateway to Lake Como, that it is easy to take a day's excursion there using public transport. Seamless boat–train connections make it even more convenient. Funiculars into the mountains give a new perspective to the Alpine backdrops, as well as adding a third means of transport to an outing.
Allow a full day.

The Duomo at Como

Trains from Milan's Stazione Nord arrive at Como's Stazione Milano Nord, near the ferry dock. Hydrofoils and slower boats ply the lake on a regular schedule, more frequently in summer when most major towns are connected twice an hour. Note that some services slow to a halt during the *mezzogiorno* – the two hours at midday when many attractions are also closed. Savvy travellers plan to join locals by eating lunch then, and strolling in parks and promenades.
Navigazione Lago di Como,
Pza Cavour. Tel: +39 (031) 579 211.
www.navigazionelaghi.it

1 Milan
Depart Milan's Stazione Nord for Como's Milano Nord station. On arrival, cross the street to the lake promenade and turn left to reach the boat landing to board a fast hydrofoil or a slower steamer for Bellagio.

2 Bellagio
From the dock, a short walk along the lake to the right leads to the gardens at **Villa Melzi** (*see p81*). To the left along the lake front, there are numerous cafés and restaurants that serve lunch, and the streets behind are filled with shops and galleries worth visiting.
Return to Como at leisure.

3 Como
From the landing, it is a short walk through Piazza Cavour to the **Duomo** (*see p78*). The promenade along the lake shore, to the right, leads through public gardens and along the marina.

4 Brunate
Alternatively, head directly to the funicular by walking left along the lake from the dock. Rising precipitously to the mountainside village of **Brunate**, the funicular has been making this 1,000m (3,280ft) climb since 1894. Over dinner or an aperitif in a terrace café at the top, you can watch the sun set and the lights come on around the lake and in Como, directly below.
Funiculare Brunate, Pza de Gasperi.
Tel: (031) 303 608. Open: daily 6am–10.30pm. Admission charge.
Return to Piazza de Gasperi via the funicular and walk along the lake to the train station for the return ride to Milan.

what to see

Como's marina, with the mountain-top village of Brunate above

Excursion: Monza

As the seat of Lombardy's government under Queen Teodolinda in the 6th century AD and Frederick Barbarossa in the 12th, and later as a country retreat for the Hapsburg rulers of Milan during the Austrian years, Monza has a royal lineage. There is no mistaking its Villa Reale for anything but a royal palace, and the cathedral is filled with reminders of its patron queen.

Monza's Duomo

Many travellers follow the royal lead, staying here to avoid both Milan's hotel prices and the high-voltage buzz of its streets. After a day in Milan, the gentle rhythms of Monza's pedestrianised central *piazze* (squares) are pleasant indeed. Alternatively, Monza makes an easy day-trip getaway for those staying in the city. Trains to and from Milan's Centrale and Garibaldi railway stations stop here at least every 30 minutes, and it's a 15-minute ride (*for accommodation see pp176–7*).

Via Italia leads from Largo Mazzini, near the railway station, through the old town centre, which retains some of its Medieval appearance. This pedestrianised street passes Piazza del Duomo, then leads to the 13th-century **Arengario**, an outstanding example of a Medieval city hall with an arcaded market at street level. Via Carlo Alberto continues north past antique shops, leading to a wooded park, the **Boschetti**. Beyond, at the southern end of the Parco di Monza, begin the grounds of Villa Reale.
Tourist Information, Pza Carducci. Tel: (039) 323 2222, www.promonza.monza.net

Open: Mon–Fri 9am–noon & 3–6pm, Sat 9am–noon.

Duomo
The best time to see the Duomo is in the late afternoon, when the stonework, pinnacles and rose window of the splendid west-facing facade catch the golden glow of the setting sun. The interior is just as arresting, with elaborate *tromp l'oeil* in its vaulting. To the left of the sanctuary, the **Cappella di Teodolinda** holds the 5th-century **Corona Ferrea**, said to contain a nail from Christ's Cross, and which crowned the kings of Italy from Medieval times through to Napoleon. Teodolinda's tomb is in the sanctuary, and scenes of her life decorate the walls of the chapel. Some of her gifts to the church, as well as her small crown, are in the **Museo Serpero**, off a small cloister reached from the centre of the nave.
Duomo open: daily 9am–noon & 3–6.30pm. Museo open: Tue–Sat 9–11.30am & 3–5.30pm, Sun 10.30am–noon & 3–5.45pm. Cappella di Teodolinda open: Tue–Sat 9–11.30am & 3–5.30pm, Sun 11.30am–noon & 3–5.45pm. Admission charge.

what to see

Palazzo Reale

The Austrian archduke decamped here from Milan to escape the summer heat, and his palace spreads grandly at the southern end of the Parco di Monza. In front is the **Roseto Niso Fumagalli**, a formal hedged rose garden and pools.
Viale Regina Margherita di Savoia. Garden open: Mon–Fri 8.30am–noon & 2–5pm, longer hours during summer, closed Aug.

Parco di Monza

Walking and bicycle trails weave their way through the wooded park and alongside the river, passing villas, tent pitches, cafés, old mills, a golf course and the **Autodromo** of Formula One racing fame. Bike rentals can be found at the southern end of the park, close to the Porta Monza.
Open: daily 7.30am–6.30pm.

Walking and cycling paths weave through Parco di Monza

what to see

Driving Tour: Val d'Aosta

The valley carved by the Dora Baltea River attracts skiers and hikers today, but in earlier times there were trade caravans and Roman legions here. Although distances are short, so much breathtaking scenery tempts travellers to linger and this excursion could easily take several days.
Follow A-4 west from Milan to A4-A5, then go north on A-5 to St Vincent. Turn north onto R-46, signposted 'Breuil-Cervenia'. Allow 2–3 days.

1 Lago Bleu and Monte Cervino (The Matterhorn)

The scenic high point is not **Breuil-Cervenia**, the ugly jumble of bunker-like hotels where cable cars begin climbing the mountain, but the magical foreground of Lago Bleu a few kilometres before town. This crystal Alpine tarn reflects the mountain in a picture-perfect scene, framed in dark larch trees. Bring a picnic and savour the moment.
Retrace your route, following S-26 west to Fenis.

2 Fenis Castle

From 13th-century origins, the castle's highlight is a charming 15th-century courtyard with a curved stairway and wooden balconies. The castle and chapel are covered in frescoes, most in excellent condition.
Tel: (0165) 764 263. www.aostavalley.com. Open: Mar–June, Sept 9am–noon & 2–6.30pm, July–Aug 9am–noon & 2–7.30pm, Oct–Feb 10am–noon & 2–4.30pm. Admission charge.
Follow S-26 west to Aosta.

3 Aosta

The Romans built a town here on their road to Gaul (France), and significant parts of it remain, including the well-preserved **Teatro Romano**, the **Arch of Augustus** (25 BC) and walls with towers and gates (*see pp12–13*). The **Museo Archaeologico** has outstanding local finds, some dating from Celtic times.
Pza Roncas 1. Tel: (0165) 238 680. Open: daily 9am–7pm. Admission charge.

The ecclesiastical complex of **Sant'Orso** packs several centuries of art into its church, bell tower, crypts and cloister. The latter is Sant'Orso's highlight, with extraordinary, intricate stone carving.
Tel: (0165) 262 026. Open: Tue–Sat 9am–7pm, Sun noon–7pm, winter Mon–Sat 9am–noon & 2–5.30pm, Sun 2–5.30pm. Turismo, Pza Chanoux 8. Tel: (0165) 236 627. Open: daily 9am–12.30pm & 2–6pm.

Five kilometres (3 miles) west, in the wine-growing village of **Sarre**, **Castello Reale** was the 'hunting lodge' of Italian King Umberto. Tours of its furnished rooms begin hourly.
Tel: (0165) 257 539. www.regione.vda.it. Cross the valley, following R-47 south, signposted 'Cogne'.

4 Gran Paradiso and Cogne

Forming Val d'Aosta's southern wall, **Parco Nazionale Del Gran Paradiso**, is a wilderness of remote valleys and rocky peaks inhabited by ibex and chamois. Attractive **Cogne**, one of its few villages, overlooks meadows of wild flowers backed by snow-capped mountains. Beyond, **Cascata di Lillaz** drops in several long waterfalls, the start of hiking trails into the park.
Tourist Information, Castello di Sarre. Tel: (0165) 257 854. www.granparadiso.net. Open: July–Aug Mon–Sat 8.30am–12.30pm & 2–6pm, Sun 8.30am–12.30pm. Closed: Dec–June Wed pm & Sun. Retrace R-47 to S-26, heading west.

5 Monte Bianco (Mont Blanc)

Monte Bianco appears ahead as a beautiful but solid wall, 50km (31 miles) long, 13km (8 miles) wide and 4,800m (15,749ft) high, blocking the end of the valley. It is hidden from the chic mountain resort of **Courmayeur**, but other imposing peaks provide Alpine decor for the designer boutiques in the village. **Museo Alpina** features early explorations of the mountains.
Pza Henry 2. Tel: (0165) 842 064. Open: Tue–Sun 9.30am–6.30pm. Admission charge. From **Entreves** beyond, aerial rides lift up to Monte Bianco's breathtaking ridge line.
ARPT, Piazzale Monte Bianco 13. Tel: (0165) 842 060.

Lake Maggiore

Despite its name, which means 'major lake', Maggiore is Italy's second largest at 65km (40 miles) long and 4km (2.5 miles) across at its widest. However, it makes up for its secondary status with knock-out good looks. Mountains surround it on all sides, sometimes dropping almost straight into its waters and elsewhere leaving a gently sloping shoreline.

Rocca Borromeo overlooks a quiet pasture

The Swiss–Italian border crosses the upper reaches of Lake Maggiore, so a day trip around the lake becomes an international expedition, even if border formalities are most often a pleasant wave through. The Italians share the lake with the Swiss, and it is a popular weekend destination for the latter; many attractions accept Swiss Francs as well as Euros.

Steamers, hydrofoils (*corse rapide*) and car ferries (*traghetti*) connect the shore towns with a frequent service, and roads circle it, rarely out of sight of the water. Towns on the southwestern shore are connected to Milan by train, while Laveno and northern points on the eastern shore are on rail lines from Garibaldi and Cadorna stations.

Cable cars of every variety carry passengers from lakeside points to the mountains around the lake for long-distance mountain views and a different perspective on the shore and lake.
Distretto Turistico, Via Principe Tomaso 70, Stresa. Tel: (0323) 304 16. www.distrettolaghi.it. Navigazione Lago Maggiore. Tel: (800) 551 801. www.navigazionelaghi.it

ANGERA

Most visitors come to the lake's southeastern corner to see the castle – and rightly so. Yet they may leave too soon, without enjoying the rest of the peninsula it occupies.

Museo dei Transporti

This open-air hotch potch of hundreds of land conveyances, from Prince Albert's 1797 phaeton to the original 1894 Brunate funicular, is possibly the most endearing and captivating museum in northern Italy. Arranged in a maze of passageways that resemble railway platforms, vehicles and related artefacts are so abundant that visitors need to look in all directions for fear of missing a horse-drawn ambulance or Pope Pius IX's railcar chapel. Follow tracks into a coal mine or descend the escalator into a subway station; museums don't get any quirkier, less high-tech – or more fun.
Off S-629, Ranco. Open: Tue–Sun 10am–noon & 2–6pm. Free admission.

Rocca Borromeo

Guarding the southern end of Lake

Maggiore since the 13th century AD, the castle once faced a sister fortress at Arona, and between them the castles controlled access to the lake. The original Medieval defensive structure remains intact, with later additions by the Visconti, from whom the Borromeos (see pp56–7) purchased it in the mid-1400s. This progression, made without destroying the original Medieval construction, makes Rocca Borromeo so worth visiting. That and the 14th-century fresco cycle in the Sala di Giustizia, depicting the battle in which the Visconti won the castle. These are considered some of the finest examples of non-sacred Medieval frescos to have survived, painted by masters at the apex of the style.

Inside the castle, the **Museo della Bambola** displays more than 1,000 dolls, and a separate building houses fashions worn by over-privileged (and probably uncomfortable) children since the 1800s.

Via alla Rocca. Tel: (0331) 931 300. www.roccaborromeo.it. Open Apr–Sept, 9am–6pm, Oct 9am–5.30pm. Admission charge.

Ranco's Museo dei Transporti is filled with early vehicles

Hikers enjoy the trails of the Fonda Toce nature reserve

SOUTHERN MAGGIORE

The most heavily visited part of the lake is this southern section which is most easily reached by train from Milan, and from nearby Malpensa airport. In this area you will also find a thicker concentration of hotels.

Arona

Arona is a good base for those arriving by train since it is well-supplied with accommodation and restaurants, and has good access to the various types of transport around the lake.
Turismo, Piazzale Duca d'Aosta. Tel: (0322) 243 601.

Arona's claim to fame – and you really should see it – is the 23.5m (75ft) tall statue of **San Carlo Borromeo**, cast in bronze and copper in 1698. One of the world's tallest statues, it commemorates the local boy who made good by becoming an abbot at age 12, and a Cardinal of Milan at 22. (A little family money and influence didn't hurt, but he was undeniably a talented cleric.) Inside the statue, 145 stairs lead to the 2.4m (8ft) head, from which one can survey the world through one eye.
Signposted from S-33, north of town. Open: daily Apr–Sept 9.15am–12.30pm & 2–6.30pm, weekends only Oct & Mar.

Fonda Toce

The wide Golfo Borromeo separates Stresa from Verbania, ending inland in the relatively undeveloped wetlands of the **Reserva Naturale di Fonda Toce**, a reed-filled bird habitat at the delta of the River Toce. Walking and bike trails criss-cross the area, and there are tent pitches inside the reserve. You can book guided walks and motorboat cruises with park naturalists at the office.
Via Canale 48, Verbania Fondatoce. Tel: (0322) 240 239. Open Mon–Fri 9am–noon & 2–5pm, Sat 9am–noon.

Stresa

Less changed by the vagaries of 21st-century economies than many other lake resorts, Stresa's impressive row of grand hotels still sparkle as they did in the Belle Epoque. The streets are lined with expensive shops, frequented by people who can afford to buy. Hemingway chose one of its luxury hotels as a setting in *A Farewell to Arms*.
Tourist Information. Pza Marconi 16. Tel: (0323) 301 150.

From Piazalle Lido, north of the centre of town, a cable car gives passengers a chance to look down at the hotels and the Borromean Islands as they ride to **Monte Mottarone**'s summit. Lakes Maggiore and Orta, the Alps and even Milan are visible from the top.
Funivia il Mottarone. Tel: (0323) 303 99, www.terradeilaghi.com. Open: daily 9.30am–6pm. Admission charge.

From a stop halfway up the cable car ride, it is a short walk to **Giardini Alpina** (Alpine Gardens), where 800 varieties of alpine plants have been gathered from mountainous regions of the world. Labelled by name and origin, they fill beds that cover a hill top. From the summer house there are striking views of the lake and islands.
Alpina. Tel: (0323) 201 63. Open: Apr–mid Oct Tue–Sun 9am–6pm. Admission charge.

Just south of Stresa, **Villa Pallavicino** has filled its park with exotic animals and birds. The formal gardens are impressive as well, planted in solid beds of colour.
Rte S-33. Tel: (0323) 315 33. www.parcozoopallavicino.it. Open: daily Mar–Oct 9am–6pm. Admission charge.

Cable cars leave Stresa's waterfront for the summit of Monte Mottarone

Boat Tour: Borromean Islands

Whether the first view of the islands in the Golfo Borromeo is from the shore, from the hills above or from a boat, the palaces, terraced gardens and jumble of stucco buildings are sights that no visitor can – or should – resist.

The schedules of the regular lake steamer make it difficult to visit all three islands in one day without feeling as though you are running a marathon. If time presses, spend more on a day ticket from one of the taxi services, which allows you to move freely and promptly, even at midday when the steamers do not stop at Isola Madre. Look for the *bigliateria* ('kiosk') next to Stresa's steamer landing.
Navigazione Lago Maggiore. Tel: (800) 551 801 (toll free). www.navigazionelaghi.it

1 Isola Madre Gardens
Almost the entire island is planted in trees, and swathes of lawn are ornamented by flower beds. The woodland walks that skirt the perimeter are open to lake views, and the entire southern shore is a terraced promenade, its vines so neatly clipped against the wall that it appears to be a hedge. Circle back up the wide walkway to the villa and admire Europe's largest Kashmir Cypress tree.
Tel: (0323) 312 61. www.borromeoturismo.it. Open Apr–Sept 9am–5.30pm, Oct 9am–5.00pm. Admission charge.

2 Villa
Signs in four languages identify art and furnishings in each room of the 16th-century manor house. While these are impressive, the house's highlights are room-sized puppet theatres and displays of marionettes and scenery.
Admission included in the entry fee for the gardens.

3 Isola Bella: Palazzo Borromeo
From the boat landing, walk left along the shore. Stop first in the chapel, opposite

From the top of the Isola Bella gardens

the entrance to see the carved marble tombs, considered the finest examples of Renaissance funerary art in Lombardy. The building of the high-baroque ancestral home of the Borromeos (still owned by the family) began in 1670, but the impressive three-storey Salon was only completed in 1948. Most astonishing is the gold and stucco Throne Room with its giant Mannerist caryatids supporting the cornice.
Tel: (0323) 305 56.
www.borromeoturismo.it. Open Apr–Sept 9am–5.30pm, Oct 9am–5.00pm. Admission charge.

4 Isola Bella Gardens

From atop the hulking and fussy wall of the Teatro Massimo (Massimo Theatre), the views down on to both sides of the Isola Bella gardens are spectacular. Patterned flower beds fall in terraces framed by sculpted evergreens. The statuary and stone flourishes make this a triumph of Italianate garden style.
Admission included in the entry fee for the palace.

5 Streets

Take time to wander in the tangle of narrow passageways leading to the shore. Classy boutiques mingle democratically with kitschy souvenir stalls, and flowering vines run amok on the walls. The lake shore is lined with cafés and eateries.

6 Isola Pescatore

Having toured the islands' sights, it is refreshing to simply wander in the stone streets and linger in the cafés of this more workaday (but equally picturesque) island, where a few fishermen still ply their trade on the lake. You can understand why Hemingway liked it here.

The Borromean Islands

CENTRAL LAKE MAGGIORE

Mountains border both shores, and recede layer after layer in the northward vistas. Some of the best views up the lake – and of the shore towns – are from the lake steamers, and even the car ferry that crosses from Intra (part of Verbania) to Laveno.
Tourismo, Corso Zanitello 6/8, Pallanza (Verbania). Tel: (0323) 503 249. Fax: (0323) 507 722.

Cannero Riviera

On a lake lined with attractive waterfront promenades, it is hard to find a more pleasant one to stroll along than Cannero's. Here there are frequent cafés overlooking the water, and a small fortified island. Hire a water taxi to see the island's castle up close.
Tel (mobile): (339) 834 3322. www.sanobanano.it

The harbour at Calde

Cannobio

Almost on the Swiss border, Cannobio is a busy little town with the curious Renaissance **Santuario della Pietà**, housing a small parchment picture with a number of miracles attributed to it. The church is right at the boat landing.
Open: 7.30am–noon & 2–7pm.

Follow brown '**Val Cannobina**' signs inland from the southern end of town to reach a deep, mysterious gorge spanned by an arched stone bridge. For views from water level, take the stone path opposite the **Oratorio Santi Anna**, which stands at the bridge. The scenic valley beyond is worth exploring if narrow mountain roads don't worry you.

Laveno

It is easy to overlook this pretty waterfront in the rush to catch the car ferry, which shortens driving distances by shuttling cars across to Intra.
Navigazione Lago Maggiore. Tel: (800) 551 801 (toll free). www.navigazionelaghi.it

A funny little bucket-like gondola lifts passengers to the summit of **Sasso del Ferro** for the stunning views. One of the lake's most photographed sights is south of the town – the lovely 13th-century hermitage **L'Eremo di Santa Caterina del Sasso Ballaro**, built into a cliff face between the villages of Cerro and Reno. Steep stone steps lead down to it.
Open: daily Apr–Oct 8.30am–noon & 2.30–6pm, Nov–Feb Sat–Sun 9am–noon & 2–6pm. Free admission.

North along the shore, the charming little harbour of **Calde** hides beneath a rock promontory. Find it by following signs to its well-known restaurant, La Vela.

what to see

Oratorio Santi Anna sits atop a deep gorge

Luino
Known chiefly for the giant Wednesday market on Piazza Garibaldi (don't even think of driving there on market day), this eastern shore town centres on a very attractive marina filled with colourful boats, which bob under the protection of a golden Madonna. The elaborate 17th-century **Oratorio dei Ss Guiseppe e Dionigi** overlooks Piazza Garibaldi.

Villa Táranto
Snuggled into Verbania's protected shore, the gardens of Villa Táranto were the passion of a retired Scottish Captain and botanist for three decades. In a land of primarily (and not surprisingly) Italianate-style gardens, the more relaxed and flowing lines of an English garden park are a nice contrast. Its formal elements – the stunning terraced garden and the avenue from the cherub fountain to the mausoleum – are set in a park filled with thousands of exotic and native trees and shrubs. More than 20,000 plant varieties, from climates as distant as the Amazonian rainforest, thrive here within sight of the pre-Alps.
Pallanza. Tel: (0323) 556 667. Open: daily Apr–Oct 8.30am–6.30pm. Admission charge.

The Borromeo Family

Generation after generation, the Borromeos have influenced art, architecture, religion and politics. Driven from Florence in 1370 after playing lead parts in a revolt, the Borromeos arrived in Milan and immediately became active members of the community.

The first of the great Lombard Borromeos was Vitaliano I, born in 1391, who became treasurer for the Duke of Milan in 1418. Selling the duke supplies, Vitaliano quickly acquired money to buy the castle at Arona and land at Cannobio, Mergozzo, Vogogna and Val Vigezzo.

When the duke's son-in-law, Francesco Sforza, inherited the dukedom, Vitaliano supported Sforzas' rule in Milan. His son, Giovanni III, managed to solve the duchy's financial woes when Sforza died in 1466 and, in gratitude, was granted more land around Lake Maggiore. Under his leadership, the family holdings became strong enough to be called the 'Borromeo State'. Giovanni became a major patron of artists and sculptors, commissioning important works.

When the conflict between the Sforzas, the Swiss, the French and the Holy Roman Empire reduced the family's influence, the Borromeos wisely withdrew to their lake territories under the leadership of Gilberto I, and worked at developing their control of the lake and its commerce. All the while, they were building Renaissance residences on the islands off Stresa, now called the Borromean Islands.

Gilberto's son, Gilberto II, married Margherita Medici, sister of Pope Pius IV (Gian Angelo Medici). Their son Carlo, born 1538, entered the church and quickly rose in its leadership in Rome. When his uncle appointed him cardinal in 1560 (at age 22) he also appointed him Archbishop of Milan. Returning there, Carlo established the first seminaries, reformed the church's administration, established synods, and began pastoral visits to his churches in response to the Protestant reformation. Carlo's younger cousin Federico also entered the church and rose quickly to the rank of cardinal as well, succeeding Carlo as Archbishop of Milan at his death. It was Federico's zeal that led to

Carlo being proclaimed Saint Carlos Borromeo in 1610.

The Cardinals Borromeo retained the family interest in art. Federico established a special committee to reconstruct and restore churches, and established the Biblioteca Ambrosiana, to which he bequeathed his personal art collection. He also erected a monumental bronze statue of his sainted uncle at the family seat of Arona (see p52).

In the mid-17th century, the family's aristocratic stature was enhanced when Carlos III's son, Renato III, married Giulia Arese, becoming the first Borromeo-Arese. A second son became a cardinal and papal legate, and the third, Vitaliano VI, was a military officer and diplomat representing Spain. A member of the Milan Council of State, Vitaliano VI was also a major benefactor of the arts and began the greatest development of the palace on Isola Bella.

His successor, Carlos IV, also followed a military and political career, serving as Viceroy of Naples and in other diplomatic roles that brought the family even wider prestige. Gilberto V successfully guided the family fortunes through the vicissitudes of the 18th-century French and Austrian occupations, as he continued construction on Isola Bella and began serious art collections for it.

With the unification of Italy in the 1860s, the family's political power began to diminish. The family still retains its long commitment to the arts, preserving the vast Borromeo collections and properties, and administering them through a trust for public benefit.

Opposite: The huge statue of San Carlo Borromeo at Ancona
Above: The Borromeo palace on Isola Bella

NORTHERN MAGGIORE

Only three boats a day travel from the southern part of the lake to Locarno, but several more leave from Luino. A hydrofoil departs from Arona at 9.30am and delivers passengers to Locarno before lunch, making this a pleasant and scenic day trip. Boat traffic is less frequent at this end of the lake, and so it is usually easier to visit the smaller towns by bus (*No 21*) from Locarno, or to drive across the border. The crossing usually involves few delays – if any at all. In either case, you will need a passport, since Switzerland is not presently a member of the EU.

Ente Turistico Lago Maggiore. Tel: (091) 791 0091. www.maggiore.ch. When calling Switzerland, use country code 0041 or +41.

Ascona

With its squeaky-clean waterfront piazza and smartly-painted buildings decked in layers of window box blooms, Ascona appears to be exactly what it is: a Swiss version of Italy. The signs are Italian, as is the cuisine, but there's a slight German accent to both, and it is a happy combination. Ascona's streets are lined by pricey boutiques and galleries – walking along these and the **Lungolago** promenade are the principal occupations of the town. In the autumn, **Settimane Musicali** brings world-renowned classical musicians to town.
Ente Turistico, Casa Serodine.
Tel: (091) 785 1965.
www.settimane-musicali.ch

Bellinzona

Castles are almost commonplace in this historical crossroads of trans-Alpine trade routes, and three overlook the town. The oldest, and most atmospheric, is the 13th-century **Castello di Montebello**, reached by passageways and stone stairs from Piazza Collegiata (a short walk from the railway station). Inside, along with battlements to walk along, is an archaeology museum.
Open: daily Mar–Nov 10am–6pm. Admission charge.

Brissago

Caught in the narrow space between mountain and lake, Brissago makes the most of its space with a kilometre-long (0.6 mile) promenade, the **Lungolago**, bordered by subtropical trees. Plants from even warmer climates grow unprotected by glasshouses on the nearby island, **Isola Brissago**, which lake waters keep at above freezing temperatures year-round. The botanical garden, begun in 1885 by a Russian

Gondola ascending Sasso del Ferro

baroness, is divided into areas corresponding with the continents where the plants are native. Medicinal plants, some extinct in their natural habitat, surround a neo-Roman bath.
Tel: (091) 791 4361. www.isolebrissago.ch. Open: daily Apr–Oct 9am–5pm. Admission charge.

Some lake steamers stop at the island and there is a more frequent service from Porto Ronco, 2km (1.2 miles) north of Brissago.

Locarno

The odd curving shape of Locarno's central **Piazza Grande** has an interesting story. The curving row of arcaded buildings follow the original building line, from when the houses rose directly from the lake. Lower water levels left the area high and dry, and it was paved with river stones to form the *piazza*. Behind its buildings rises an area of twisted narrow streets, arcades and garden-filled courtyards. Step through the archways to see Medieval houses, fountains and lush gardens, especially in **Piazzetta de'Capitani**, **Piazzetta delle Corporazione**, **Casa del Negromante** and **Casa dei Canonici**, which has a Medieval garden.

Near the railway station, a *funicolare* (funicular railway) carries passengers to **Orselina** for views and access to a *funivia* (cable car) bound for even higher **Cardada**. Locarno is the starting point for the scenic Centovalli train excursion (*see pp174–5*).

Piazza Grande once formed Locarno's shoreline

Excursion: Lake Varese

Overshadowed by larger lakes, Lake Varese and the region that surrounds it are rich in fascinating sights but little known to foreign tourists. A Medieval mountain-top town enlivened by modern frescoes, a 5th-century archaeological site, a holy mountain and the quiet reedy lake shore with its birdlife and nature preserve all await the curious traveller. The attractive old town of Azzate makes a good centre from which to explore the region (*see pp176–7*).
Tourist Information Centre, *Pza Liberta 1, Varese. Tel: (0332) 252 031.*

Arcumeggia

The narrow road to Arcumeggia winds upwards alarmingly to reach a cluster of Medieval stone buildings and roughly cobbled passageways. Not at all the 'murals for tourists' one would expect, these mid-20th-century paintings are small, their colours subdued and their subjects diverse, ranging from religious

Palazzo Estense from the gardens

Fresco at Arcumeggia

themes to a bicycle race. No boutiques or souvenir shops mar the scene, and only two eating places await visitors.
Follow S-394 from Laveno to Cittiglio, turning left to Casalzuigno, from which the Arcumeggia road branches to the left.

At the turning in Casalzuigno, **Villa della Porta Besozzo** stands in a splendid baroque garden set around a wide terraced staircase with stone balustrades and statuary. The original 1500s' farmhouse was transformed into a grand villa with the addition of 18th-century frescoes and rococo interior details.
Tel: (0332) 624 136. Villa open: Oct–Nov Tue–Sun 10am–1pm & 2–5pm, Feb–Sept Tue–Sun 10am–1pm & 2–6pm. Park open: Oct–Nov 10am–5pm, Feb–Sept 10am–6pm. Admission charge.

Castel Seprio

The walls and foundations of a 5th-century basilica, and portions of even earlier stone towers and houses show a

village destroyed in 1285, when Milan and Torino fought for control of the region. An excellent free booklet in English maps and describes the village, through which visitors can walk, although it is an active archaeological sight. Also at the site is the 8th-century church of **Santa Maria Foris Portas**, with Byzantine frescoes.
Via Castelvecchio. Tel: (0331) 820 438. Open: Feb–Oct Tue–Sat 8.30am–7.30pm, Sun 9.30am–6.30pm. Closes: earlier Nov–Jan. Free admission.

Castiglione Olona

This rather ordinary town has a most surprising corner tucked into a ravine at one side. Looking more Tuscan than Lombardian, the enclave was the work of a local cardinal who spent much of his life in Florence as a papal legate. Returning to Lombardy, he began reshaping his village by reworking his family villa, **Palazzo Branda Castiglioni** (*Piazza Garibaldi. Tel: (0331) 858 048. Open: Tue–Sat 9.30am–12.30pm & 3–5.30pm, Sun 3–5.30pm, Apr–Sept also Sun am. Admission charge*). The **Collegiata** church at the top of the hill has outstanding Renaissance frescoes in the baptistery, but the artistic ideas of the time are unfettered in the **Chiese di Villa**, opposite the *palazzo* (*open: Tue–Sun 10am–noon & 2.30–5.30pm. Admission charge*).

Varese

Parks and terraced formal gardens surround the richly decorated former villa of the d'Este family, **Palazzo Estense**, built in the 1700s and which Stendahl called 'Versailles in Milan' (*Open: Mon–Sat 10am–noon & 2–6.30pm*). In **Campo dei Fiori** park, north of the town, is **Sacro Monte di Varese**, an ascending series of 17th-century chapels with larger than life figures depicting biblical scenes.

The village of Castel Seprio was destroyed in Medieval times

Lago d'Orta

Wooded hillsides embrace little Lake Orta, only 13km (8 miles) long and barely 2km (1.2 miles) at its widest. The road around its shore is 33km (21 miles) long. What it lacks in size it makes up for in beauty, with a Medieval town at its centre and a little island of garden villas just offshore. It's enough to make even the most dedicated non-photographer wish for a camera.

Boats for Isola San Giulio

Isola San Giulio is in the lake near Orta San Giulio

what to see

Transportation between lake towns and to the island is provided by Navigazione Lago d'Orta. (*Tel: (0322) 844 862. Operates daily Easter–mid Oct, Oct–Nov Sat–Sun*) and Servizio Pubblico Motoscafi Lago d'Orta (*Pza Motta. Tel: (333) 605 0288. www.motoscafipubblici.com*).

Isola San Giulio
The centrepiece of the tiny island is its excellent Romanesque **Basilica di San Guilio**, founded in the 4th century AD and rebuilt in the 9th and 10th. Stone-carved reliefs and columns date from this era, and the campanile was added in the 12th century. Inside is a 12th-century pulpit of Oira marble, carved in unusual designs. *Tel: (032) 290 358. Open: daily in summer, Tue–Sun in winter.*

Legend holds that the church was founded by San Giulio, who drove away the snakes (and a dragon, according to some stories) to make the island habitable. In the crypt is his sarcophagus. From the monastery, **Via del Silenzio** leads to the shore, with signs apprising walkers to uphold the virtues of silence.

Omegna

By comparison to spiffed-up Medieval Orta San Giulio (see below), Omegna is the plain-Jane cousin. However, it is not without charms, sitting at the outlet of the lake against a soaring mountainside. Flower boxes line the riverside and bridge, and a Thursday market fills the tree-shaded lake front. A nine-arched loggia forms a porch on the Palazzo di Citt, where the tourist office is located.

Omegna's main industry is the manufacture of quality kitchen utensils and cookware, and several companies are based here. **Forum Omegna** is a striking modern showcase for these products, with a museum, café and a shop selling products of Calderoni, Lagostina and others (*Parco Rodari. Tel: (0323) 866 141. www.forumomegna.org Open: Tue–Sat 10.30am–12.30pm & 3–7pm, Sun 10.30am–12.30pm. Free admission*). Lagostina has its own outlet shop of fine cookware at discounted prices (*Via Novembre 39. Tel: (0323) 652 255. Open Tue–Sat 9am–noon & 3–7pm, Mon 3–7pm*).

Orta San Giulio

Clustered tightly on the shore, from above Orta appears as a solid block of grey stone and red tile. No cars are allowed in the narrow streets, so visitors descend into this Medieval town on foot via one of the winding lanes, under overhanging balconies. Via Olina is the main street, running parallel to the lake shore until it reaches the café-encircled expanse of Piazza Motta. Here a new dimension is added to the scene – the deep blue of Orta's waters and the picture-perfect island just off shore. At the water's edge are boats waiting to ferry passengers across.

The frescoed, 16th-century Palazzo Communita stands above a loggia at one end, and behind the café tables are smart boutiques and artisans' studios which extend into the side streets. This is a town to wander around, taking your time. Above the town, and reached either by car or a steep path from Piazza Motta, is **Sacra Monte**, one of several 'sacred mountains' in this region. Inside a nature reserve of beech, pine and lime tree forests, 20 chapels with terracotta scenes from the life of St Francis line a path through the woods. The church San Nicolao and the chapels, built from 1591 to 1770, contain frescoes and 376 statues.

A small tourism office in the 'new' town hall, near the lake shore, has a

Omegna sits at the head of the lake

Old town hall fresco, Orta San Giulio

leaflet describing walking routes around the lake. (In the courtyard there is often a display of sculpture by local artists.) The regional tourist information is at the first car park, above the town.
Tourist Information, Via Panoramica. Tel: (0322) 905 163. Open: Mon–Fri 9am–1pm & 2–6pm.

Pettenasco
A short distance north of Orta San Giulio, Pettenasco lies between the road and the shore. Its tall, Romanesque church tower, visible from the main road from either direction, was once part of the church but was left on its own when the new church was built in the 1700s. The **Museo dall'Arte della Tornitura del Legno** displays various tools and products from the town's woodworking past.
Via Vittorio Veneto. Tel: (0323) 896 22. Open: June–Sept Tue–Sun 10am–noon & 2–6pm. Free admission.

what to see

Lago di Lugano

The steep, wooded slopes of Lugano's shore leave room for fewer towns than on Como and Maggiore. Relatively small, at 35km (22 miles) long and 3km (1.8 miles) at its widest, the lake winds in and out of Switzerland, where it is known as Lago Ceresio, with either end in Italy. Most of its tourism is in the central Swiss section. Remember that calls to Swiss locations from abroad are preceded with country code 41.

Lugano's lakeside promenade

LUGANO

Like an amphitheatre, Lugano rises from the lake front in a bowl shape, parts of the old town so steep that streets become staircases. Its location protects it from harsh alpine weather, but connects it by rail with the Swiss cities of the north and Milan to the south. An express bus links to Malpensa airport (*www.busexpress.com*).
Tourismo di Lugano, Riva Albertolli. Tel: (091) 911 3232. Fax: (091) 922 7653. www.lugano-tourism.ch. Open: Apr–Oct Mon–Fri 9am–6.30pm, Sat 9am–noon, Sun 10am–2pm, Nov–Mar Mon–Fri 9am–12 noon & 2–5pm. A kiosk at the railway station is open Mar–Nov, Tue–Sun 2–7pm.

Centro Storico

The old streets and arched passageways which radiate from Piazza della Reforma are lined with shops where smartly-dressed shoppers laden with designer boutique bags mingle with housewives choosing the perfect porcini from little markets that spill out into the streets. A market fills Piazza della Reforma every Tuesday and Friday morning, and at almost any time you can watch men pondering their next move on the giant chess board in the adjoining Piazza Manzoni.

Lungolago

Curving languidly around the shore is the tree-shaded Lungolago, a promenade with benches overlooking the water and the mountains. It connects

what to see

the two landing piers for excursion boats – Paradiso at the south end, and the main dock opposite Piazza della Reforma. About halfway between the two, **Giardino Belvedere** provides a green interlude, with rose gardens and flower beds interspersed with sculpture.

Monte Bre

The forested mountain framing the left-hand side of Lugano's Lungolago view is the 933m (3,061ft) high Monte Bre. You can easily ascend to see lake views, an art trail and a village of traditional houses. To reach the funicular, take the No 12 bus from waterfront to the Cassarate/Monte Bre stop. *Operates: daily 9.15–11.45am & 1.45–4.15pm, June 15–Sept 9.15am–4.45pm, every 12 minutes.*

Monte San Salvadore

Within walking distance of the Paradiso boat landing and railway station, one of Europe's oldest funiculars ascends the 912m (2,992ft) tall Monte San Salvadore. Views open in every direction, sweeping both arms of the lake, Lake Maggiore and a panorama of the Swiss/Italian Alps. Picnic at the top or visit the **Museo San Salvadore**, with minerals, fossils and ecclesiastical art (*Open: Wed–Sun 10am–noon & 1–3pm. Free admission*). A footpath leads to the settlement of Ciona, atop a neighbouring mountain. (*Operates: Mar–Nov, every 30 minutes until 11pm.*)

Santa Maria degli Angioli

The region's finest example of Renaissance art is Bernardino Luini's monumental *Crucifixion*. The fresco, painted in 1525, shows the crucifixion with scenes from the life of Christ. He used his wife as a model, and his own face for a Roman soldier. Artists could not sign works in churches, and so such hidden 'signatures' were used.

Lake Lugano from Monte San Salvadore

Boat Tour: Lake Lugano

A trio of interesting towns lie along the lake close to Lugano, each easy to visit by boat. Unfortunately, they are divided among two routes, one connecting Gandria and another Morcote and Campione d'Italia.

Casino at Campione d'Italia

It is possible – with an early start – to combine both trips in the same day and still have time to enjoy some of the shore sights. The trick is to begin by going south to Morcote, skipping Campione and changing boats at the Paradiso landing, where both lines stop, instead of at the main Lugano port. However, it is better to plan one circuit each day or to choose only one. Returns are also possible by local bus.
Navigazione del Lago di Lugano.
Tel: (091) 923 1779. www.lakelugano.ch

An alternative option is to book a private lake tour by vintage mahogany boat, replete with tales of smuggling. The Castelnuovo brothers (*Tel: (091) 967 2013*) know the subject well since their father was a smuggler.

Campione d'Italia

This little enclave of Italy, surrounded by Switzerland on all sides, has an understandably split personality. Vehicles have Swiss licence plates and phones use the Swiss code, yet the official currency is the Euro and laws are Italian. The famed *maestri campionese* originated here – a team of architects, artists and sculptors whose church-building skills spread the Lombard style throughout Italy and Europe, rivals of the *maestri comacini* (*see p76*).

Overlooking the shore at the south end of town, **Santa Maria dei Ghirli** is a small chapel with an important 17th-century fresco cycle by Bianchi and elaborate embellishments. The early 8th-century church of San Zeno, now the **Galleria Civica** used for exhibits, has its original frescoes. But most tourists don't come to see the churches; they come to gamble at the casino and enjoy the lively nightlife in the town's many cafés and restaurants.
Tourist Information, Via Volta 16.
Tel: (091) 649 5051.

Gandria

Steps and narrow passages lead between the close-set houses on the narrow shelf where the town clings. Cantine di Gandria, reached from lake, is known for its cosy *grotti* – the traditional little restaurants. **Museo delle Dogane Svizzere** (Customs Museum) is in the former lake customs post at the Swiss/Italian border, and shows boats seized in the act of smuggling.
Tel: (091) 910 4811.
www.musee-suisse.ch. Open: daily Palm Sun–Oct 1.30–5.30pm. Free admission.

Morcote

An arcade covers the street along the shore, and antique shops, booksellers

Santa Maria del Sasso overlooks Morcote and Lake Lugano

and restaurants hide beneath it, making the picturesque little town a pleasant place to stroll. Above, the hillside church of **Santa Maria del Sasso** is well worth the climb for views down into town which, from that perspective, give a geometric design of roof tiles against aqua-blue water. The church contains some of the region's best 15th-century frescoes, in particular the medallions in the cross vaults and under the arches.

Parco Scherrer is a trip around the world inside a hillside garden. The garden designs, plants, statues, fountains and even buildings reflect times and places from Renaissance Ticino to the Far East. Scherrer collected plants and ideas wherever he travelled, and the result is surprisingly harmonious, seamlessly blending a Thai teahouse, a Greek temple, a little Indian palace and an Egyptian temple each in its own native flora.

Tel: (091) 996 2125. Open: mid Mar–Oct 10am–5pm, June–Aug until 6pm. Admission charge.

Train Tour: Centovalli

One of Europe's most scenic train rides connects Lake Maggiore's northern shore in Switzerland's Ricino region, with Domodossola, at the foot of the Simplon pass. The Centovalli (One Hundred Valleys) railway follows the Melezza River and its tributaries, each of which has carved a valley of its own. The 52km (32 mile) railway line, completed in 1928, crosses 83 bridges and passes through 31 tunnels. Vintage railway carriages feature polished wooden interiors and windows that open for photography. *Allow 2 hours for train ride, full day for hikes or excursions.*

Two alternatives allow travellers to tailor the trip to their own tastes. An out-and-back trip on the Centovalli line provides time for activities – hiking or exploring small mountain villages. A loop itinerary combining both boat and train gives more variety, but less time to get off the train and explore.

From any point on Lake Maggiore it is possible to take a boat to Locarno, where the train trip begins. From Domodossola, travellers can board the Trenitalia for Stresa, catching a boat back to their starting point. Combined excursion tickets make this easy, and Rail Europe passes are valid on the Centovalli.

First-class passengers can pre-book a substantial lunch of local salamis and cheeses with bread, fruit and wine, or a trolley offers sandwiches. Those planning to explore mountain towns can plan to visit on a market day and buy provisions for a picnic there.

1 Locarno
The trip begins at the railway station, a short walk from the steamer landing (*see pp58–9*). The train emerges from a tunnel onto a terrace overlooking vines.

2 Intragna
The Ticino's tallest church spire marks the entrance to the Centovalli here.

Lake Palagnedra from the train

From the impressive iron bridge, look back to see an old Roman bridge below. A *funivia* carries passengers to the mountain village of Costa, a 20-minute ride away (*Tel: (091) 756 0400. Operates: daily Mar–mid Nov 9am–12.40pm & 2.30–6.10pm, every 20 minutes*). Intragna has a small museum of mountain crafts and folklore.

3 Verdasio
Another cable car (*Tel: (091) 756 0400. Operates: daily Mar–mid Nov 9am–12.40pm & 2.40–6pm, every 20 minutes*) travels across a valley to a high plateau and the village of Rasa, which is accessed only by footpath or cable car. A spectacular trail leads downward to Costa (*about 2.5 hours*), from which a *funivia* returns to Intragna. This requires taking the local train from Locarno, or disembarking at Verdasio, where the Centovalli excursion trains do not stop, to ride two stops on the next local train, always 20 minutes later.

4 Camedo
This is the last Swiss stop; Italian border patrols will board to check passports.

5 Re
The domed pilgrimage church is filled with votive offerings to the image of the Madonna, which locals reported seeing bleed after someone threw a rock at her forehead. Saturday is market day.

6 Santa Maria Maggiore
The highest point on the trip, Santa Maria is popular with artists, whose galleries line the streets. The town hall has frescoes and decorative stucco work, and a museum of chimney sweeps tells of a traditional local employment. Monday is market day.

7 Domodossola
The Centovalli trip ends at the railway station, where passengers can connect to the Trenitalia for Stresa or return via the same route with different, east-bound views.

Lake Como

Wealthy Romans decamped from steamy lowlands to the cool of Como's shores, building the first of the lake's long succession of villas. By the 1800s, the lake had become the favourite watering hole of the rich and famous, especially for the British, who continue to favour Como, perhaps the most beautiful of all Italy's lakes.

Paddleboat rental on Lake Como

Long (46km (28.5 miles)) and narrow (650m (2,133ft) to 4.2km (2.5 miles)), and shaped like an inverted 'Y', Como cuts a deep gash into the mountains that rise steeply on either side. Snow-clad alpine peaks reflect in the sapphire waters, and the mountains provide a barrier protecting the lakeside from both the harsh Alpine climate and from the frequently murky skies of the Venetian plain. Even in winter, Lake Como is temperate, its shores clothed in green and its afternoons often warm enough for tables to be set outdoors on terrace cafés.

Pastel-painted villages climb the steep shores, often looking as though they had been arranged there by an artist, who finished the picture by painting green all around them. An astonishing array of villas enjoy these views, and although few are open, many of their gardens, designed to frame these vistas, are open for strolling. Flowers bloom everywhere, especially in the Tremezzina Riviera.

Explore the lakeside villages on foot to find narrow passages hung with flowering vines. Many buildings rise right from the water, often with arcaded watergates and tiny marinas of their own.

The Romans founded Como as a post on the trade route across the Alps, making it an important crossroads between the Mediterranean, Adriatic and Northern Europe. Its former status is best shown by the work of its outstanding school of artists and architects, the *maestri comacini*, whose intricate stone carving is found in churches scattered throughout Northern Italy, and worth looking for in even the most modest village churches here.

Roads hug both shores (at frightening altitudes on the section from Como to Bellagio), but the frequent ferry service by both hydrofoils and slower steamers is a good alternative for visiting most of the lakeside towns. Distances are short, and a day's excursion can combine several towns, with time to look around each and to visit attractions. From a base near the centre of the lake, it is very easy to reach all its corners. Many attractions are within walking distance of the ferry landing. Economical day passes allow multiple stops.

Navigazione Lago di Como, Pza Cavour. Tel: +39 (031) 579 211. www.navigazionelaghi.it

Regular trains and buses connect Malpensa and Linate Airports to Milan's

what to see

77

Stazione Centrale, from which trains run twice each hour to Como, a ride of about 40 minutes. Shuttle trains from Milan's Stazione Nord arrive at Como's more centrally located Stazione Milano Nord, near the ferry dock, and are timed to meet the ferries. A direct bus from the adjoining bus station connects to Malpensa Airport.

LEONARDO TO *STAR WARS*

Como's glamorous scenery and extravagant villas have not escaped the attention of artists seeking the right setting. Leonardo da Vinci, who stayed on Lake Como in the late 1400s, used its landscapes as backgrounds for some of his best-known paintings, including *Madonna and Saint Ann*. More recently the loggia of Villa Balbianello became the wedding venue for Queen Amidala in *Star Wars*.

Excursion boats leave regularly from Como

COMO

With the lake and mountains beckoning enticingly, it's easy for visitors to hop on to the first boat without stopping to admire the city. That would be a mistake. Not only is Como a pleasant blend of busy small city and vintage tourist haven, it also has an outstanding, if exuberant, Duomo.

The historic and touristic central section hugs the shore in a warren of streets, all of which seem to lead eventually to the wide and walkable waterside promenade. Café-lined Piazza Cavour is at its centre, near the starting point for passenger boats. *Como APT (tourist information centre), Pza Cavour 17. Tel: (031) 274 064, (031) 269 712. www.lakecomo.com. Open: Mon–Sat 9am–1pm & 2–6pm. A smaller kiosk is located on the south side of the Duomo.*

Duomo

Nowhere in Italy can you see a better example of how, in the 14th century, Gothic morphed into Renaissance. In the Duomo, Gothic origins are immediately clear in the richly ornamented marble facade, carved pinnacles reaching skywards and carved figures flanking the entrance. Do note these, for they are not the expected saints, but effigies of the Roman Plinys, both natives. By the 1500s, perhaps everyone had forgotten Pliny the Younger's correspondence with Emperor Trajan suggesting reasons for executing Christians. Inside, Gothic elements include the beautiful rose window and deeply carved altarpieces. The St Ambrose altarpiece, in the first chapel on the right, shows the transition from medieval (it's carved in stone) to Renaissance (the polychrome painting). In the next chapel is Luino's *Adoration of the Magi*, one of three Luinos in the cathedral.

Piazza del Duomo. Tel: (031) 265 244. Open: daily 8am–noon & 3–7pm. Free admission.

Tempio Voltiano in Como

Museo Civico

From Neolithic artefacts uncovered nearby to memorabilia from the World Wars, the Museo Archeologico and the Museo Storico fill two former *pallazi* with an illuminating picture of the Como region from its earliest history. Roman relics remind visitors that the city's walls were built by order of Julius Caesar. More contemporary eras are covered in exhibits about the work of Garibaldi in unifying Italy.

Via Vittorio Emanuele. Tel: (39) 031 271 343. Open: Tue–Sat 9.30am–12.30pm & 2–5pm, Sun 10am–1pm. Admission charge.

Sant'Abbondio

See the work of the stonemasons, the *maestri comacini* (*see p72*), in their home town at this outstanding Romanesque church. Its high naves, reminiscent of paleo-Christian churches, are decorated with intricate stone carvings and 13th-century Gothic fresco cycles that transform the apse and are still bright and lively. Note that this is a dingy part of town.
Via Regina (no phone). Open: daily 8am–6pm. Free admission. Bus No 4 or 7 as far as main train station.

Notable on Como's lake front **Promenade** (well worth strolling) is the white **Tempio Voltiano**, memorial to native son Alessandro Volta, whose name gives us the word electric 'volt' (he invented the battery). Near it, almost hidden in a garden, is the sobering and eloquent **Holocaust Memorial**, with quotes from victims in several languages. Further on to the west, the shore is dominated by **Villa Olmo**, whose extensive gardens are a public park. At the opposite end, a funicular ascends to mountain-top **Brunate** (*see p82*).
Funiculare Brunate, Pza de Gasperi. Tel: (031) 303 608. Open: daily 6am–10.30pm. Admission charge.

Gardens at Villa Olmo overlook Lake Como

An old Lake Como gondola at Villa Melzi d'Eril

BELLAGIO
Possibly the most perfect setting on Lake Como is reserved for Bellagio, whose streets and gardens rise on the triangular promontory at the centre of the lake's distinctive 'Y' shape. Not exactly undiscovered, Bellagio is well aware of how picturesque it is, but its appeal remains undiminished. Perched on its terraces and lining its narrow streets, candy-coloured buildings house boutiques and cafés, with facing streets that sometimes become staircases. More cafés offer lake views along the waterfront. This is a good place to while away a day or so, with plenty of sightseeing to keep you from feeling lazy.

Bellagio's position at the centre of Lake Como makes it an ideal (if pricey) base for exploring, with boat connections to all three arms of the lake and car ferries shuttling to either shore.
Bellagio Tourist Information, Lungolago Mazzini. Tel: (031) 950 204. www.bellagiolakecomo.com. Open: Apr–Oct daily 9am–noon & 3–6pm. Closed: Nov–Mar Tue & Sun.

Basilica di San Giacomo
Above the busy shopping streets, in the historic part of town, the 12th-century basilica is remarkable for its detailed stone carving by Como artisans, known as the *maestri comacini* (see p76). Their work can be seen in the capitals of the

columns in the nave, and in the fine stonework of the apse.
Pza della Duomo. Open: 8am–noon & 3–7pm.

Villa Melzi d'Eril
Although the neo-classical villa's interior frescoes are not on public view, its English-style gardens are lovely to walk through. Azaleas and rhododendrons are stunning in the spring, and stately cypresses and exotic plants frame lake views and hide a Japanese garden. A neo-Moorish pavilion sits on the shoreline, and a small chapel and pavilion with changing art exhibits are open to visitors.
Lungolario Marconi (south on S-583). Tel: (02) 8699 8647. Open: daily Apr–Oct 9am–6pm. Admission charge.

Villa Serbelloni
A lane behind the Basilica di San Giacomo leads to the villa's gardens, set in a park which crowns the promontory. Italianate 19th-century-style landscaping uses exotic trees as a stage set for views across northern Lake Como, which is backed by snow-capped Alps. Roses are barely contained between prim box hedges.
Pza della Duomo. Tel: (031) 950 204. Garden tours: mid Apr–Oct Tue–Sun 11am & 4pm by reservation, book at the tourist information office in Bellagio. Admission charge.

The little fishing village of **Pescallo**, the oldest settlement on this peninsula, is a pleasant 20-minute walk from Bellagio, with waterside cafés and *trattorie* (restaurants). For a more strenuous hour's hike with a rewarding view of all three branches of the lake, climb to the belvedere at **Mulini del Perlo**. Walk a little further to **Chevio-Makalle** for another panorama. By car, follow the narrow mountain roads to San Primo, where you can ride the cable car up **Monte San Primo,** or climb to the summit from the end of the road. Winter visitors can ski there.

Many of Bellagio's streets are stairways

WALKING AROUND COMO

Dedicated (or even casual) walkers will find paths everywhere which lead to fascinating sights missed by other travellers. An excellent pack of cards, *By Foot in the Province of Como*, with each card detailing a complete walk (in English), is available from provincial tourist offices. With these you can find huge boulders dropped by glaciers, castle ruins, waterfalls, Roman roads and Iron Age rock engravings.

SOUTHERN LAKE COMO

The lake's western arm begins at the city of Como and includes some of its least-visited towns. Discouraging vehicles from travelling between Como and Bellagio is the vertiginous road, in places barely wide enough for two cars.

Brunate

Rising at grades as steep as 55 per cent, a century-old funicular climbs more than 1,000m (3,281ft) from Como's lake front to give fantastic views of the lake and mountains. Café terraces in the precipitous village offer views to the south, but to see the Alps and the lake shore towns to the north, you must climb the stone-paved path to the tower at the top. Once there, to save climbing the 143 tower steps, enjoy the same view in comfort from a café table at La Regonda.

Funiculare Brunate, Pza de Gasperi. Tel: (031) 303 608. Open: daily 6am–10.30pm. Admission charge.

Cernobbio

The S-340 road follows Como's western shore to Cernobbio, whose lake front is dominated by villas. The most elegant of these is **Villa d'Este**, designed in the late 16th century by Pellegrino Tibaldi. Formerly home of English Queen Caroline, it is now a sumptuous hotel, surrounded by elaborate Italianate gardens. **Parco Villa Erba**'s gardens are open to the public on weekends.
Via Regina 2. Tel: (031) 34 91. Open: Sat 2–6pm & Sun 10am–6pm. Free admission.

North of town is the road to **Monta Bisbino**, a 1,355m (4,446ft) tall mountain with a road to its summit and spectacular panoramas of both Italy and Switzerland. The Swiss boundary is near the mountain top. Just beyond the turn-off is **Moltrasio**, known for its gardens and the 11th-century church of **Sant Agata**.
Tourist Information, Via Regina 33, Cernobbio. Tel: (031) 510 198.

Nesso

Unless you catch a quick glimpse of the arched stone bridge as you pass through Nesso on S-583, you might not be tempted to stop. But those who have first seen Nesso from the lake steamer's infrequent stops know that far below the road is one of the loveliest vignettes on the lake. Follow the steeply descending cobbled streets and stone stairs along the south side of the deep rocky ravine, which slices the town in half, to emerge

Villa d'Este's elaborate gardens

what to see

Nesso sits astride a deep gorge with a Roman bridge at its foot

at lake level. Here, centuries-old stone buildings rise out of the water, and the Nose River is spanned by a **Roman bridge**. Deep inside the ravine there is a long waterfall.

Unfortunately the boats do not stop here but at the town docks further north, from which you must climb to road level before descending again into the cleft. Nevertheless, they do pass tantalisingly close for good, if fleeting, views of this enchanting spot.

Just south is **Careno,** a tiny moss-covered stone settlement clinging to the steep lake shore. The Romanesque church of **San Martino** is reached by a steep path from the road above.

Torno

This Medieval village at a bend in the lake is known for **Villa Pliniana**, built in the 16th century at the spot where Pliny the Younger had earlier built a villa. A cascade there still turns on and off at regular six-hour intervals, just as Pliny described it. Stop at the church of **San Tecla** to see its outstanding Romanesque carved portal.

THE TREMEZZINA RIVIERA

The mildest shores of this calm-weather lake are along the central western shore, in an area known as the Tremezzina Riviera. Lush foliage encases the hillsides and wraps itself around the villas. Palms, camellias and exotic trees thrive here, many of them far north of their usual range. Like Bellagio, this makes a good central base from which to explore by car or boat, with frequent steamer and hydrofoil services and a car ferry connecting to Bellagio in the centre and Varenna on the eastern shore.
Tremezzo Information, Via Regina 3. Tel: (0344) 404 93. www.tremezzina.com Open: May–Sept Mon–Wed, Fri–Sat 9am–noon & 3.30–6.30pm.

Villa Balbianello

Spread luxuriantly across the end of a peninsula are the immaculately groomed grounds of a baroque villa, built for Cardinal Durini in the 1700s. Lawns slope gently down towards the lake, bounded by a sculpted stone fence, from whose top rail life-sized statues gaze across the lake. Each massive tree and blossoming shrub is placed to frame the lake and mountain views. Lake steamers pass close enough for an enticing preview of the villa from the water. Like other gardens in the region, these are at their most flamboyant from late April through to mid-June, when azaleas and rhododendrons are in full bloom. But with or without the flowers, Villa Balbianello and its gardens are considered to be the lake's most romantic.

Visits to the gardens begin in nearby Lenno, from where boats depart during the garden's opening hours. It is also possible to visit the gardens on foot (it is less than a kilometre's walk (0.6 mile)) from Lenno on Tuesdays, Saturdays, Sundays and holidays.
Tel: (0344) 561 10. Open: Apr–Oct Tue, Thur, Fri 10am–1pm, 2–6pm, Sat–Sun 10am–6pm. Admission charge.

Also in Lenno is the 11th-century church dedicated to **Santo Stefano**, which has an interesting Romanesque baptistery and a crypt where parts of a fine Roman villa have been discovered. In 1945, Mussolini and his mistress were killed in **Mezzegra**, a short distance inland, after their capture at Dongo on the northern shore of Lake Como.

Villa Carlotta is known for its gardens

what to see

Villa Carlotta

Taking full advantage of the Tremezzina's mild temperatures, Villa Carlotta, an 18th-century palace built for the Prussian Princess Carlotta, has one of Northern Italy's most celebrated gardens. Originally planted in the 1850s, its camellias, rhododendrons, azaleas and exotic trees line broad paths, and open to a succession of lake views backed by mountains. Although the 5.6 hectares (14 acres) of gardens are the best reason for visiting, the villa itself is open as a museum of sculpture (with several pieces by Canova) and paintings by the Lombard masters. Its furnished rooms and interior decorations are 18th century.

Via del Paradiso. Tel: (0344) 404 05. www.villacarlotta.it. Open: daily Apr–Sept 9am–6pm, Mar and Oct 9–11am & 2–4.30pm. Admission charge.

The villa is on the way to Cadenabbia, just north of Tremezzo, an easy, pleasant walk along the shore promenade – an occasionally interrupted alley of plane trees known as **Via del Paradiso**. Up the hill in Griante is the cone-topped church of **San Martino**, set on a scenic terrace overlooking the lake.

Tremezzo's lakeside is a pleasant place to walk

Isola Comacina

A great deal more is unknown about the troubled and eventful history of Isola Comacina than is known. Throughout its story weaves a who's who of famous names – Frederick Barbarossa, Queen Theodolinda, King Albert of Belgium, Vittorio Emanuele's daughter and saints Abonde, Agrippa and Domenica.

Frequent boats travel to Isola Comacina

The island seems to have been a hotbed of religious fervour, as the presence of three saints would attest. By the time the barbarian hordes swooped in from the east, the tiny island already had five churches on it, at least one thought to have been a temple built by the Romans and subsequently consecrated by Christians.

Certainly Comacina was inhabited in Roman times, and probably long before that, since its steep shore was easily defended. At the arrival of the first barbarians, wealthy Christians escaping Como took refuge here, naming it Christopolis and waiting out the attacks of Atilla the Hun and the Goths who succeeded him.

When the Lombards conquered Northern Italy in the 6th century, the Byzantine governor managed to escape to Isola Comacina, bringing with him his considerable treasure and reinforcing its fortifications. This aroused the interest of the husband of Lombard Queen Theodolinda, who besieged and conquered the island, sparing its inhabitants but seizing the treasure.

In turn, the Lombard King Berenger II took refuge there in 962 AD, as did the Holy Roman Emperor Frederick Barbarossa in the 12th century. The island became known as a place of refuge, even peace, and Sant Abbondio and at least two others found hermitage there. It was Abonde who brought the cult of Santa Eufemia to the island, and initiated the building of the largest church, a basilica dedicated to her.

The islanders' unwise siding with Milan in the rivalry between Como and Milan was their undoing. Although Milan eventually won out, Como was the closer neighbour and razed the island in 1169. They were not so generous to the inhabitants, who were either killed or fled. The ruins of that attack are what we see today on the now deserted island.

Touring the island

A single trail loops around the island. Following it uphill leads along the crest of the highest point, and to the foundations of **Santa Maria col Portico**, with olive trees growing among its stones. Beyond here the trail descends to reveal the best view of the remaining group of churches. Of the Medieval **Basilica di Santa Eufemia**, low walls and

Ruins of Basilica di Santa Eufemia below the island's only remaining church

stone floors remain to show its layout in a little glen below the later baroque **Oratorio di Santi Giovanni, Pietro e Paulo**, still standing.

Easy to miss behind the oratorio is the **paleo-Christian baptistery**, with mosaics from the 5th–9th centuries and frescoes from the time of Charlemagne, in geometric patterns. The island is an atmospheric place to take a picnic lunch and to wander with ghosts from the Middle Ages.

Boats shuttle back and forth from Sala Comacina, where there is ample parking uphill from S-340.
Tel: (0338) 459 9492. Operating: daily Mar–Oct 9am–midnight. Or the regular lake steamers stop at the island. Navigazione Lago di Como. Tel: (031) 579 211. www.navigazionelaghi.it

NORTHERN LAKE COMO

The landscape becomes less precipitous along the northern shore of the lake. Some of the most interesting attractions – a 13th-century abbey and a deep chasm carved in solid rock – are in this region.

Orrido di Bellano

Abbazia di Piona

The 13th-century abbey surrounds a fine Romanesque cloister, showing the beginnings of the Gothic style. Delicate columns end in capitals with detailed carving in a wide variety of motifs. Frescoes date from the 14th and 15th centuries, and more cover the sanctuary of the adjoining 11th-century church of San Nicola. Cistercian monks at the active monastery grow medicinal herbs and produce the cosmetic creams, honey and liqueurs sold in the shop.
Open: daily 8.30am–12.30pm & 1.30–7pm. Free admission.

Bellano

The most outstanding natural wonder on Lake Como is the long and convoluted **Orrido di Bellano**, a deep gorge sculpted into potholes and caves by the River Pioverna. Seen from the safety of walkways high above river level, the gorge has a waterfall in its centre.
Tel: (338) 325 7117. Open: daily Apr–Sept 10am–12.30pm & 2–11pm, Oct– Mar Sat–Sun 10am–12.30pm & 2–7pm.

Beside the steps leading to the Orrido stands the early Gothic church of **Santi Nazaro e Celso**. The mid-1300s' facade of striped stone features a rose window. The frescoes in the nave are remarkable examples of *tromp l'oeil*, fooling the eye into seeing flat walls as statuary, balustrades and relief carving.

Gravedona

One of Lombardy's major Romanesque sites, the 12th-century church of **Santa Maria del Tiglio**, has a free-standing octagonal bell tower, with early frescoes of St John the Baptist and a section of floor revealing mosaics from the 5th-

Cloister of Abbazia di Piona

century previous structure. The inside of the tower is completely open and almost severe, the large fragments of fresco giving an inspiring impression of how it must have looked when the entire interior was covered with them.
Via Roma. Open: Mon–Fri 3–5pm, Sat–Sun 10am–6pm. Free admission.

Menaggio
Smart cafés surround the lakeside Piazza Garibaldi in the historic centre of this attractive resort. Less geriatric than the Tremezzina, Menaggio has a better selection of restaurants. The road to **Lake Lugano** climbs (stop for lake views at **Croce**), then levels out to Portelezza. Just north, in the village of Nobiallo, **Santuario della Madonna della Pace** sits tranquilly among olive and cypress trees, perhaps the loveliest setting of any church on the lake.

Varenna
Clustered under cliffs, Varenna appears from the lake to be a geometric pattern of pink, red, gold, cream and ochre stucco with a green surround. A lakeside promenade bordered with bright flowers connects the ferry landing to the town centre. The convent of **Villa Monastero**, abandoned in the 16th century, provides terraces of formal gardens filled with Mediterranean and exotic plants.
Tel: (0341) 295 450. www.villamonastero.it. Open: daily 9am–noon & 2–7pm (5pm off-season).

Above the city, the 11th-century **Castello di Vezio** has a falconer and falcons demonstrating this Medieval art.
Via Esino Lario. Tel: (0335) 465 186. www.castellodivezio.it. Open: daily Apr–Oct 10am–6pm, later during June–Sept, Nov–Mar weekends only. Admission charge.

Medieval frescoes at Santa Maria del Tiglio

Agri-tourism

Farmhouse bed and breakfasts, country restaurants that serve meals made from home-grown ingredients, bee-keepers with roadside kiosks, horse-riding ranches, farms with camping sites – all these small rural enterprises are promoted in Italy under the banner of *agriturismo* (agri-tourism). The initiative is a happy one for those travellers who delight in meeting local people and eating wholesome local dishes.

Added to this is the knowledge that the money spent helps to maintain a way of life which is often endangered in the modern world. Frequently, this extra income from tourists provides the margin to keep a family farm alive. Some enterprises may seem no more than a crowded backyard garden, but it may surprise you to learn how self-sufficient a family can be on a small plot of land.

Each region has its own directory of these establishments, and those with guest rooms are listed in the back pages of local accommodation guides. The range of activities you can enjoy at farms is wide. Some invite you to take part by milking the cow or helping in the grape harvest, although you are never expected to work unless you wish to. All will enjoy sharing the workings of their operation – a tour of the barns, a walk in the orchard or vineyard, a pony ride for the kids, or the opportunity to watch milk become cheese. And you may be sent off with a bag of freshly picked cherries, a jar of honey or a sausage from the smokehouse.

Rooms may be simple and comfortable, either in a section of the farmhouse or in a purpose-built inn on the property. Alternatively, you may find yourself in a vintage family villa, especially in the rich farmlands of the Mantova region. These are often a distance from towns with restaurants, and so many provide a hearty farmhouse dinner in the evening, or have a full restaurant of their own. All include breakfast, and you can depend on the fruit jams being homemade.

Often situated at the end of country lanes, these farms may be tricky to find, but if you book in advance they will send maps, or you can ask at the nearest village if you miss a signpost.

For illustrated directories of properties, including restaurants, accommodation and farm shops, contact the following agencies:
APT del Mantova (tourist information centre), *Pza Mantegna 6.*
Tel: (0376) 328 253.
Fax: (0376) 363 292.
Associazione Agriturismo Trentino, Via J Aconcio 13, 38100 Trento.
Tel: (0461) 235 323.
Fax: (0461) 235 333.
www.trentinoagritur.it
Regione Lombardia Direzione Generale Attivita Produttive – Servizio Promozione, Via Sassetti 32, 20124 Milano.
Fax: (02) 676 562 94.
www.lombardia-agriturismo.com

Agriturist Veneto, Via Monteverdi 15, I-30170 Venezia Mestre.
Tel: (04) 292 249.
Fax: (04) 292 456.

Agriturismo Fioravante A small Valpolicella winery, close to Verona. *Via Don C Biasi 7, 37020 San Floriano, Verona. Tel: (045) 770 1317. Fax: (045) 770 1317.*

Camping Clarke Camping site on a small farm with horses, other animals and fresh eggs, south of Bellagio. *Localita Visgnola. Tel: (031) 951 325.*

Locanda Mose High above Lake Como, with guest rooms, camping site and a restaurant specialising in products of the farm, which include ricotta and freshly picked berries. *Localita Pian di Nesso. Tel: (031) 917 909. Open: all year. Closed: Wed.*

Opposite: Agri-tourism sign in Angera
Above: Agriturismo Fioravante
Below: Entrance to a farm guest house near Lake Garda

what to see

Bergamo

Bergamo has a decidedly split personality. The new city spreads on the flat plain while, above it all, the regal old city – the Città Alta – is encased in high walls. The lower city is only new by comparison: it was built after the Medieval and Renaissance streets and *piazze* of the upper city.

Frescoes decorate Bergamo's churches

At the centre of Bergamo's Città Alta is a beautiful ensemble of Renaissance buildings around a sloping *piazza*, and through the loggia at the top is another *piazza* surrounded by churches and related buildings. Cutting through the centre of the old city, Via Gombito is a narrow Medieval lane lined by shops, churches and tiny squares. Most of the city's prime sites are in this old hill top town.
Tourist Information, Vicolo Aquila Nera 2 (off Pza Vecchia). Tel: (035) 232 730. Open: daily 9am–noon & 2–5.30pm.

Funicular

This is the easiest and fastest way to get from Viale Vittorio Emanuele, in the Città Bassa at the foot of the hill, to Piazza Mercato delle Scarpe in the Città Alta, the old town at the top of the hill. It runs on rails and is pulled by dual cables, rising at an ever-increasing gradient through the massive walls.
Viale Vittorio Emanuele II. Tel: (035) 364222. Open: mid June–mid Sept 7am–1.30am, closing at midnight the rest of the year. Tickets are valid for

the funicular and any bus fare in the same zone for an hour.

Pinacoteca Accademia Carrera

The generous Giacomo Carrera gave not only his entire collection of paintings to the city in 1796, but the neo-classical building as well. With the addition of other collections, the Accademia now houses more than 1,600 paintings and other collections of sculpture, drawings, prints, medals, porcelains and bronzes. Look for everything from Angelico and Botticelli to Pisanello, Rubens, Raphael and Van Dyck. The gallery covers three floors, with the primary collections housed on the second and third floors. There are seven closed rooms on the first floor containing about 600 paintings which can be seen by request. Adjacent is the **Galleria D'Arte Moderna E Contemporanea** dedicated to the visual arts of the 20th century. It concentrates on Italian artists, but also has works of non-Italians. The collections include De Cherico, Kandinsky, Morandi, Bale and Casorati.
Pza Giacomo Carrera 82A. Tel: (035) 399 643. www.accademiacarrera.bergamo.it. Open: Apr–Sept Tue–Sun 10am–1pm & 3–6.45pm, Oct–Mar Tue–Sun 9.30am–1pm & 2.30–5.45pm. Admission charge.

La Rocca

Bergamo's Castle is a hard, uphill walk but well worth it for the view over the old town alone. Site of the Roman Capitolium, the castle was begun in 1331 and finished by the Visconti in 1336. Blown up in 1511 by lightning and again by the French, it was later possessed by the Venetians and the Austrians, serving as a prison and place of execution for Garibaldi's followers until he liberated it in 1858. World War I armaments are found in a courtyard. A former military school in the grounds used to be a museum of the Risorgimento but has been closed, and is expected to reopen as a museum of the two World Wars.
Piazzale Brigata Legnano. Tel: (035) 224 700. www.museostoricobg.org. Grounds open during daylight hours. Museums temporarily closed.

Bergamo's Città Alta sits above the newer town

PIAZZETTA DUOMO

The small square behind Piazza Vecchia – the Piazzetta Duomo – and the adjoining Piazza Giuliani contain a trove of Bergamo's treasures. This is the probable site of the Roman Forum and the medieval 'People's Assembly', and it is now flanked by the cathedral and a clutch of other ecclesiastical buildings.

Aula della Curia

Upon entering this hall, you will be transported to the 13th century. The arch and all of the frescoes date from that period, and the whole ensemble is intact. The building served as the entry hall to the diocesan curia. *Enter from either Via San Salvatore or Pza Vecchia.*

Baptistery

Originally inside the basilica of Santa Maria Maggiore, the 14th-century baptistery was taken down after 1659 and put away in storage. Two hundred years later it was reassembled, with a slightly altered roof. Dissatisfaction with its location led to its second disassembly and reconstruction here in 1898, this time with a heightened base. Slender columns line its octagonal top, along with eight 14th-century statues of the virtues. The font with bas-relief of the life of Christ in the centre is also octagonal, and is by Giovanni da Campione.

Colleoni Chapel

Next to the north portico of the basilica stands the late Gothic Colleoni Chapel, the mausoleum of Bartolomeo Colleoni who was a 15th-century *condottiere*, the protector of Venetian interests in the area. Designed by Giovanni Amadeo, much of the exterior sculptural work is also by him. Inside, the tomb reflects the outsized ego of the warrior/lord. The frescoes are by Giovan Battista Tiepolo, and were completed in 1733. The tomb of Bartolomeo Colleoni's 15-year-old daughter, Medea, was moved here in the 19th century.
Tel: (035) 210 061. Open: Apr–Oct Tue–Sun 9am–12.30pm & 2.30–6.30pm, Nov–Mar 9am–12.30pm & 2.30–4.30pm.

Duomo

The neo-classic facade of the cathedral of Sant'Alessandro dates from 1886, but the interior is baroque. To the left of the door is Moroni's *Madonna and Child*,

The portico of Santa Maria Maggiore

and on the main altar, the second painting to the left is the Tiepolo *Martyrdom of St John, Bishop.* Tel: (035) 210 223. Open: daily 7.30–11.45am & 3–6pm.

Santa Maria Maggiore

Begun in 1137, the basilica is considered one of the finest Romanesque works. The main entrance in red, white and black marble is the work of Giovanni Campione. A loggia holds a mounted Saint Alexander flanked by two saints; the smaller loggia above was added in 1396. Along the walls to the left is a minor portal topped by a crucifix also by Campione, as is the south portico, a tall arched canopy supported on columns that rest on the backs of standing lions and crouched telamons. Above is a frieze of Christ and twelve apostles, with saints on the side. The iron strips affixed to the walls were medieval units of measure. Inside, the outstanding wood inlay work on the presbytery stalls is by Lorenzo Lotto, one of the masters of inlay.
Tel: (035) 223 327. Open: Apr–Oct Mon–Sat 9am–12.30pm & 2.30–6pm, Sun 9am–12.45pm & 3–6pm, Nov–Mar Mon–Sat 9am–12.30pm & 2.30–5pm, Sun 9–12.45pm & 3–6pm.

The Gothic Colleoni Chapel

Tempietto di Santa Croce

Opposite the southern entrance of Santa Maria Maggiore, this is a tiny gem of Romanesque architecture. It was built in the 10th century and restored in 1561. *Via San Salvatore. Tel: (035) 237 279. Open: by appointment, exterior always visible.*

Contarini Fountain in Piazza Vecchia

Musei Civico

There are actually three civic museums in Bergamo. Two are situated in the Piazza della Cittadella near the western end of Viale Mura, approached through the 1355 **Torre della Campanella** (Tower of the Little Bell). Inside the courtyard is the **Museo Archeologico** with a collection of artefacts dating from prehistoric through to Lombard times. Off the same courtyard is the **Museo Civico di Scienzi Naturali**. It has extensive collections of specimens, more than 10,000 lepidoptera, an herbarium with 4,000 species, fossils (including the flying dinosaur reptile *eudimorphodon Ranzii*) and a reconstructed mastodon. The **Museo Storico Della Città** presents the history of Bergamo through its artefacts.
Archeologico and Scienzi Naturali.
Viale Mura at Pza della Cittadella. Archaeology Tel: (035) 286 011. Natural Sciences Tel: (035) 242 839. www.museionline.it. Both open: Apr–Sept Tue–Fri 9am–12.30pm & 2.30–8pm, Sat–Sun 9am–7pm, Oct–Mar Tue–Sun 9am–12.30pm & 2.30–6pm. Storico. Pza Mercato del Fieno 6. Tel: (035) 247 116. Open: Apr–Sept Tue–Fri 9.30am–1pm & 2–5.30pm, Sat–Sun 9am–7pm, Oct–Mar Tue–Sun 9.30am–1pm & 2–5.30pm. Admission charge.

Museo Donizettiano

The great opera composer Gaetano Donizetti lived and worked here in Bergamo, and the two rooms of an 18th-century palace memorialise his life. His nearby birthplace, which shows the poverty from which he ascended, can be seen by appointment.
Via Arena 9. Tel: (035) 399 269. www.museostoricobg.org/donizetti/doniz htm. Open: Apr–Sept Tue–Sun 10am–1pm & 2.30–5pm, Oct–Mar Tue–Sun 10am–1pm. Birthplace: Via Borgo Canale 9. Open: by appointment.

Piazza Vecchia

This is about as close to a perfect Renaissance square as will be found anywhere. In the 15th century, a warren of buildings was removed and the civic building, the 12th-century **Palazzo Ragione,** was rebuilt to face the new square. Its covered staircase was added in 1453, and the loggia in 1520. The main room has significant 13th-century frescoes, but is open only during exhibitions. The tall clock tower in the corner (**Torre Civica** or **Il Campanone**)

what to see

dates from the 12th century and was a Ghibelline stronghold (*see pp98–9*). The clock still rings curfew at 10pm. Along the western side is the 1340 Palazzo Podesta, former home of the Venetian Governor. At the north end is the white, marble-faced **Civica Bibliotecha A. Mai**, housing 1,274 incunabula among its collections. In the centre is the beautiful **Contarini Fountain** presented to the city in 1780, with fantastic lions, serpents and sphinxes.
At the intersection of Via Gombito and Via Colleoni. Torre. Open: daily May–Sept 8am–10pm, Oct Sat–Sun 10am–6pm, Nov–Feb Sat–Sun 10.30am–4pm, Mar–Apr Tue–Fri 10am–12.30pm & 2–6pm.

Viale Mura and the Gates
Use Viale Vittorio Emanuele II for the best road access to the Città Alta. At the end there is one of the original gates to the walled city, **Porta Sant'Agostino**. Inside the gate, **Viale Mura** begins, running inside the town wall on the eastern, southern and western sides. Immediately at the right of the gate is the convent of Saint Augustine which is used for exhibitions, and a large promenade created in the 1880s. Straight ahead, Viale Mura turns into Via Della Fara and leads to **Porta Di San Lorenzo**, the gate through which Garibaldi entered the city.

On the southern side, about midway along Viale Mura, is another gate – **Porta Sant Giacomo**. Viale Mura meets up with Via Tre Armi, which runs at the foot of the hill, at its western end at **Porta Sant'Alessandro**.

A café sits under the loggia on Piazza Vecchia

The Venetian Empire: Looking for Lions

The symbol of St Mark is the lion, and both the saint and his symbol are inextricably tied to Venice and the Venetian empire, which stretched across Northern Italy to include Brescia and Bergamo. Although the boundaries of the present-day Veneto have receded somewhat and the region begins at the western shore of Lake Garda, traces of the lion remain in the lands once controlled by *La Serenissima* – the Venetian Republic.

The lion often stood atop a column, as he does in Verona's Piazza dell Erbe. However, these types of lion have disappeared outside the Veneto region, and you are more likely to find the lion carved in bas-relief on a prominent wall overlooking a square, or on the arch over a gate.

The Venetian lion is easy to distinguish from just any old lions that might embellish a fountain, or guard an entrance. First, he is winged and he always holds (or originally held, if the carving has been damaged) a book in one paw. If the book is open, Venice was at peace when he was carved there. When the book is closed, Venice was at war.

Many of these lions have gone, some deliberately defaced or removed when the Venetians left town. Others have fallen victim to war, neglect or development. Yet a non-violent form of lion hunting will turn them up, sometimes in unexpected places such as carved on a pulpit. Scan old *piazze* and the courtyards of Medieval and Renaissance town halls. In Brescia's Broletto (*see p106*) you can see where a lion has been almost entirely defaced.

Bergamo retains a classic lion of St Mark at the main entrance to the old city, where the street passed through Porta Agostino (*see p97*). Above the gate, a large lion is carved, open book in paw. At night, when the gate is bathed in floodlights, you can see it from the lower town. In Rovereto (*see pp130–1*), St Mark's lion on the old city gate reminded those who entered that they were in a city of *La Serenissima*.

Also in Bergamo, a relief panel of the lion of St Mark faces the Piazza Vecchia, a prime example of how these were placed to remind the populace of who was in control.

Another clue that a city was once Venetian – or at least had a strong Venetian influence – is a triple set of arched windows, separated by delicate columns. Look for these on Brescia's Broletto and the building surrounding the clock tower in Piazza Loggia. In Mantova you will see them on one wing of the Ducal palace. The style is very common in Verona, where you will see these windows on many buildings, but especially in Piazza degli Signori (*see p136*). You can find this style in the towns around Lake Garda as well.

Opposite: If the book in the lion's paw is open, Venice was at peace when he was carved
Above: Venetian-style windows face the Duomo in Brescia

what to see

Excursion: San Pellegrino and the Val Brembana

Few places evoke the Belle Epoque, in all its fading grandeur, quite like the spa town of San Pellegrino. The springs of this town are the source of the world-famous water, whose familiar label shows the turreted spa that made the town a mecca for the rich and famous in the early 20th century.

The Casino at San Pellegrino

Although the grandest of the hotels have closed, enough remains of the architecture, the splendour and the spa's easy ambience to reward a trip there. And for anyone who loves Art Nouveau architecture, this town rates a gold star on the map of Europe.

The valley in which San Pellegrino lies, the Val Brembana, is pretty itself, although the river scenery is marred with hydro-power plants below San Pellegrino. Some distance up the valley beyond, the road snakes up the Passo San Marco, the only road to scale that wall of mountains. Centuries of traders have followed this tortuous route, but the mountains are now the realm of hikers, climbers and skiers.

The whole region is filled with small farms, many of which welcome visitors to buy their fresh baked goods, wines, cheese and fruit.

San Pellegrino

After an unpromising entrance to the town, past the enormous bottling plant for the famous mineral water, the S-470 becomes San Pellegrino's main street. The town climbs the hill on the western bank of the Bremba, connected by a wide bridge to the Art Nouveau railway station and the massive Grand Hotel.

The hotel, stucco crumbling and with its great wrought-iron canopy rusting away, stands brooding over the river. If an antiques show or other exposition is happening there, seize the chance to see the interior, where an enormous spider chandelier hangs in the entrance hall, and the stucco work and ceilings are in surprisingly good condition.

Opposite, San Pellegrino has fared the vicissitudes of fashion better, its arcaded buildings in good repair, and the town is lively with cafés and shops. Behind and above is the casino, with its towers and stone frills. Reached through well-kept gardens, a wide terrace fronts the casino, theatre and arcaded Terme San Pellegrino, the spa.

The facade of the casino is decorated with every imaginable embellishment and the inside of this astonishing wall of stonework is no less amazing – an entrance hall in textbook Art Nouveau. The walls are stencilled in the familiar floral scroll panels, and every detail is in period. But this pales beside the grand salon ahead, where a split staircase rises into an almost hysterical outburst of decoration, featuring every motif and medium Art Nouveau style.

The spa is still operating, both in the elegant old building adjoining the casino, with its wall fountains, and in the stylish modern spa across the street below. You can drink from the springs, swim in the elegant pool, take the cure for gout or indulge in therapeutic baths, wraps and massages.

Via Taramelli 2. Tel: (0345) 224 55. www.sanpellegrino.it. Open: Tue–Sun 8am–noon & 3.30–6.30pm. Pool open: Tue–Sun 11am–7pm. Admission charge.

The grand salon of the casino is the epitome of Art Nouveau

what to see

Lago d'Iseo

West of Lake Garda and easily reached from both Bergamo and Brescia, Lake Iseo has been a summer haven for the cities' noble families, who built villas on its shore. Before that it was a centre of commerce with the north, and home to fishermen.

Iseo's Lungolago Marconi

Although often maligned for the industry at its shore (mixed manufacturing), which is in fact confined to cities at either end of the lake, Iseo still has most of its shore intact. In the north, vertical limestone cliffs drop into the water, and along the southern shore is a nature reserve known for its profusion of water lilies, which bloom spectacularly in the spring.

The claim to fame for this small lake is the mountain that rises out of its centre, forming a cone-shaped island. The castle-topped mountain – Monte Isola – is the largest freshwater island in Europe. Also outstanding are the hundreds of prehistoric pictographs in the Val Camonica, north of the lake, which are protected by a National Park.

A 60km (36 mile) road encircles the lake, whose towns can also be reached by ferries and tour boats with dining facilities, operated by Gestione Navigazione Lago D'Iseo. *Via Nazionale 16, Costa Volpino. Tel: (0359) 714 83. Fax: (0359) 729 70.*

You can reach Lake Iseo from Bergamo or Rovato (on the main Milan–Venice train line) via the **Treno Blu**, a tourist railroad that runs to Sarnico where it links with the boats for a tour of the

what to see

lake and Monte Isola. A day excursion includes train, boat to Monte Isola, and lunch.
Tel: (0354) 243 937. www.ferrovieturistiche.it Buy tickets on-board or at **Clio Viaggi**, *Via G. d'Alanzo, Bergamo.*
Tel: (035) 233 031. Fax: (035) 248 023.

Capo di Ponte

The human occupation of the **Valle Comonica**, north of the lake, dates at least from the Bronze Age, and is demonstrated by the hundreds of images carved into the rocks by prehistoric peoples. **Parco Nazionale delle Incisioni Rupestri** protects a huge mountainside area of these at **Capo di Ponte**. Incised in the exposed rocks, which are well-connected by pathways, are deer, labyrinths, ladders, hunters and alphabets. A map with descriptive information is available in English. The little museum describes what is known of the lives of prehistoric peoples through dioramas and artefacts. Parking is along S-42, with a trail up to the park. In the off-peak seasons, there is parking closer to the entrance.
S-42. Tel: (0364) 421 40. Open: Mar–mid Oct Tue–Sun 8.30am–7.30pm. Admission charge.

Rock art at Capo di Ponte

The Romanesque **Monasterio di San Salvatore**, built in the 11th and 12th centuries, has beautiful stone carving, as does Capo di Ponte's parish church of **San Siro**, also 11th-century Romanesque.
Monasterio di San Salvatore, Capo di Ponte. Open: daily 9am–noon, 3–6pm. Admission charge.

Clusane

On the southern shore, west of Iseo, Clusane is a small and attractive fishing port known for its restaurants specialising in lake fish. Looming over the shore is the boxy **Castello del Carmagnola**.

The harbour at Clusane

Monte Isola is the largest lake island in Europe

Iseo

Since the pre-Christian era – at least as far back as 400 BC when Celtic peoples inhabited the area – Iseo was an important trading centre for goods produced by the entire region. Since prehistoric times the Camonica Valley, north of the lake, was a busy highway and, until a shoreline road and a railroad were built in the 19th century, the lake carried traffic from the valley to Iseo. Today it is the headquarters for tourism, with its compact town centring on Piazza Garibaldi. The beautiful **Lungolago Marconi** is a promenade around the shore, with views of the lake, cafés, and it is a favourite spot for local shore fishermen. *Azienda Promozione Turistica, Lungolago Marconi 2. Tel: (030) 981 361. Open: Mon–Sat 9am–12.30pm & 3.30–6.30pm, Sun 9am–12.30pm.*

Castello Olfredi, now housing the town's cultural centre and library, dates from the 11th century but was rebuilt in the 14th (*Via Mirolte. Open: Mon–Fri 9am–noon & 2–5pm*). The 12th-century church of **Sant'Andrea** has an original Lombard Romanesque bell tower, and the tomb of Giacomo Olfredi is built into its outside wall.

Monte Isola

In the middle of Lake Iseo, Monte Isola is the largest lake island in Europe, and has retained its air of an insular fishing community possibly because no private vehicles can go there. A small bus connects the towns, which lie among vineyards and groves of chestnut and olive trees. The 14th-century **Rocca Martinengo** (north of Sensole) and another **Castello Olfredi** (outside Peschiera Maraglio) once protected the island. The church of **Santa Maria della Ceriola** is a pilgrimage site because of a venerated wooden statue of Mary. On the top of the mountain, it can be reached by bus from Cure in the summer.

Fishing and fish curing are still active industries on the island. You can visit the curing houses and perhaps see people making or mending fishing nets.

The island fishing cooperative offers boat tours from Sulzano that include visits to a shop which makes fishing nets, a wooden boat builder, and a close-up look at the two small, privately-owned islands near Monte Isola.
Barcaioli Piccola Societá Cooperativa, Monte Isola. Tel: (0347) 819 9172/ (0335) 844 0916. Open: by appointment.

The island has good hiking trails and narrow roads where cyclists do not have to contend with traffic. A ferry service to Peschiera Maraglia and Sensole operates from Sulzano, on Lago d'Iseo's eastern shore. Ferries to Carzano leave from Sale Marasino. Both are frequent.
Ufficio Turistico Peschiera, Peschiera Maraglio. Tel: (0309) 825 088.

Pisogne

At the northern end of the lake, Pisogne is a small town with attractive arcaded buildings. On the road towards Fraine, the former monastery of **Santa Maria della Neve** has an outstanding cycle of frescoes by one of the region's best-known artists, Girolamo Romani (Romanino). Locals call this 'the poor man's Cistine Chapel'.
Tel: (0364) 870 32. Open: Tue–Fri 3–5pm, Sat–Sun 9.45–11.30am. If closed, ask at the Romanino Bar next door.

San Pietro in Lamas

Off the old road south of Iseo, overlooking the lake and nature reserve west of Iseo, is the 12th-century monastery of San Pietro in Lamas. Along with its setting and views, it is worth visiting for its fine 15th-century frescoes.
Provaglio D'Iseo. Tel: (030) 983 477.

Fishing in Lake Iseo

Brescia

An often overlooked city, Brescia was one of the earliest Roman settlements in the north. Its sights, from the ancient forum to its Novecento Piazza Vittoria, show more than two millennia of architecture and art. Particularly informative, free brochures, which highlight subjects such as churches and Roman sites, are available from the tourist office.

Pza Loggia 6. Tel: (030) 240 0357. www.bresciaholiday.com Open: Apr–Sept Mon–Sat 9.30am–6.30pm, Oct–Mar Mon–Fri 9.30am–12.30pm & 2–5pm, Sat 9.30am–12.30pm.

Interior of Duomo Nuovo

Broletto

The centre of public life while Brescia was a city state, the Broletto remained in this role when the Venetians took over in the 15th century. Still in government service, three sides of its internal courtyard are medieval and one side has a 17th-century colonnade.

Pza Paolo VI, across from the Duomo. Courtyard open: normal workdays.

Capitolium and the Piazza del Foro

Brixia, as the Romans called it, was by the 1st century AD a major city filled with important buildings. In its forum, Vespasian erected the Capitolium in AD 73, but it was destroyed by fire in the 5th century. Rediscovered in 1823, it was partially reconstructed in 1939. Original components of white marble in the columns and pediment are easy to distinguish from the brick used in reconstructed parts. Portions of the arcaded forum have been excavated to reveal former Roman shop fronts, and while you cannot wander around in these, everything is clearly visible.

Via Museo, Pza Foro.

Castello

Atop Cidneo Hill, where the Celts once built their town, the castle offers

Restored Capitolium

spectacular views over the city. Thick brick walls tower over a dry moat and the tall, round Prisoner's Tower commands the entrance. Inside, the former Venetian grain storage is now the **Museo dell Risorgimento**, dedicated to the period of Italian unification. The Visconti Keep houses the **Civico Museo delle Armi Luigi Marzoli**. Its ten rooms, some with 14th-century frescoes, hold an incredible collection of Italian and European arms from the 14th to the 18th centuries.
Cidneo Hill (by car from Piazza Cesare Battisti or Pza Arnoldo). Castle open: daily 8am–8pm. Museo Armi and Museo Risorgimento open: June–Sept Tue–Sun 9am–5pm, Oct–May 9.30am–1pm & 2.30–5pm. Admission charge.

Civici Musei d'Arte e Storia Santa Giulia

Newly and beautifully created in the former convent of San Giulia, this is the home of Roman Brixia. The treasure trove of Roman antiquities includes a Winged Victory (actually a 3rd-century BC Greek piece), mosaic floors, fragments of columns, and other decorative detail that was uncovered during extensive excavations. The interior of two 1st-century Roman houses include frescoed walls and mosaic floors. This new municipal museum brings together a tremendous wealth of other artefacts from the city's history, brilliantly interpreted and displayed.
Via Musei 81b. Tel: (800) 762 811/ (030) 297 7834.
www.bresciaholiday.com/santagiulia.
Open: June–Sept Tue–Sun 10am–6pm, Sat 10am–7pm, shorter hours in winter.

Decumanus Maximus

Brixia's forum was located on the Decumanus Maximus, the most important city road. At the foot of the stairs leading to the Capitolium, a section of the original road has been exposed, where it runs past the arcaded fronts of Roman shops.
Via Museo, Pza Foro.

Roman Brescia exhibit at the Civici Musei

Duomo Nuovo

This is the 'New Cathedral', but new is relative. The church was begun in the 17th century, the huge cupola completed in the early 19th century. The last altar on the right wall is the tomb of Sant Apollonio and has an excellent Last Supper painted on wood below. Under the dome, the four gospel apostles appear with their symbols.
Pza Paolo VI. Tel: (030) 427 14. Open: Mon–Sat 7.30am–noon & 4–7.30pm, Sun 8am–1pm & 4–7.30pm.

Duomo Vecchio

Next door is the Romanesque 'Old Cathedral' from the 12th century, with 9th- and 11th-century crypt and Medieval frescoes. This is one of the few round, early Christian churches remaining intact. In its rotunda, eight trapezoidal pilasters manage to support the cupola. A number of 16th- and 17th-century paintings by Romanino, Moretto and Francesco Maffei can be found in the chapels.
Pza Paolo VI. Tel: (030) 427 14. Open: Apr–Oct Tue–Sun 9am–noon & 3–7pm, Nov–Mar Sat–Sun 9am–noon & 3–6pm.

Piazza del Foro

This *piazza* covers the site of the forum – the focus of city life during the period of Roman rule from roughly the 1st century BC until the 5th century AD. Here, the Roman road Decumano Massimo (now Via Museo) and its next most important street, Cardo Massimo (Via Cereto), met. At the top of the *piazza* are the Capitolium and the church of San Zeno In Foro (18th century).

Brescia's Romanesque Duomo Vecchio

Piazza Loggia is an elegant Renaissance square

Piazza Loggia

Only a short walk from the Piazza Vittoria, Piazza Loggia provides a great contrast. While Piazza Vittoria is an entire ensemble of Novecento, or Facist, architecture, entering Piazza Loggia is like stepping into the Renaissance, an open expanse with arcaded buildings at either end. It is named for the 15th-century Palazzo Loggia, in whose design both Sansovino and Palladio had a hand. The unusual roof was added in 1914, allegedly designed after a period print. Across the piazza is the Torre del'Orologio (Clock Tower) in a Venetian arcaded building from the 15th century. Two human figures strike the 1518 bell. The tourist information office is in the old Monti Pieta (Pawnbrokers), an attractive 16th-century building.

Pinacoteca Civica Tosio Martinengo

The gallery is housed in the 15th-century Martinengo palazzo with a collection by 13th- to 18th-century Italian painters, including a fine collection of major Bresian artists. There are works by Raphael, Veneziano, Solario, Lotto, Romanino and Moretto. Many of the works were originally in churches and private collections.
Via M da Barco, Pza Moretto.
Tel: (030) 377 4999. Open: June–Sept Tue–Sun 10am–5pm, Oct–May Tue–Sun 9.30am–1pm & 2.30–5pm.
Admission charge.

Teatro Romano

Excavations of Roman Brescia continue, and at the east end of the Capitolium is the Flavian-period (AD 69–96) Roman theatre, which originally sat 15,000 people. In its upper section was a brick ambulatory, and below a hall of pillars still joins it to the Capitolium. Much of the theatre's seating remains, as well as parts of the underpinnings of the stage area.
Not open to the public but visible from Vicolo Fontanone.

Walk: Brescia

Brescia's two millennia of sights are neatly packaged into two clusters, connected by a street that follows the ancient Roman main road. A parking garage is hidden under Piazza Vittoria, making it a good place to begin, even though it means walking backwards through history.
Allow 2 hours walking time, plus stops.

Start in Piazza Vittoria.

1 Piazza Vittoria
A complete square of Novecento (Fascist) buildings, the *piazza* includes an often overlooked detail of the era, a balcony for addressing crowds, this one is an unusual red, marble carved 'pulpit'.
Walk to the right of the striped postal building, following Via Post through the arch.

2 Piazza Loggia
Imbedded into the southern wall are stones from earlier Roman buildings, which were put there in 1480. There is a distinctly Venetian look to the building with the clock tower, atop which two *Macc de le ure* (crazy timekeepers) ring out hours (*see p109*).
Walk through the arch under the clock, bearing right.

3 Broletto
On your left in Piazza Paolo VI (named for Brescian Pope Paul VI) are the 13th-century tower and government buildings of the city state (*see p106*).

4 Duomo Nuovo and Duomo Vecchio
Beyond the Broletto are these two cathedrals, side by side. This is unusual, since new cathedrals were so often built on top of the earlier ones (*see p108*).
Leave the piazza from the end you entered, going right through the arch and arcaded courtyard of the Broletto. Turn left onto Via Mazzini, then right onto Via dei Musei.

5 Via dei Musei
Following the Roman high street, Decumanus Maximus (parts of which lie buried beneath), the street is lined

Clock tower on Piazza Loggia

what to see

with *palazzi*. Stop at the courtyard of Palazzo Martengo Cesaresco, on the right. Churches on this street have brown historical signs in English.
Continue to Piazza del Foro.

6 Capitolium

Standing above the forum, the temple has been reconstructed to show four of its six columns and much of its pediment. A segment of original street and parts of the forum are excavated (*see p106*). You can admire this ensemble from the conveniently placed tables of Caffè Caligola.
Turn left at the end of the excavated area.

7 Teatro Romano

Built into the hillside (parts of which buried it in a landslide), much of the amphitheatre is visible (*see p109*).
Follow Via Fontanone to the right, turning right again to rejoin Via dei Musei, heading left.

8 Civici Musei d'Arte e Storia Santa Giulia

Inside former convent grounds, the new museum of art and history has excavated two rooms of a major Roman house, over which the convent was built in AD 753 by Desiderius, King of the Lombards (*see p107*).
Retrace your steps to Via Piamarta, turning right.

9 San Cristo

Two other churches are incorporated into the complex, and the facade of one is visible from Via Piamarta. This 15th-century monastery has a pretty cloister and interesting marble carvings on its portal. More carvings are found on the outside of the apse behind the church, and inside it is richly frescoed.
Return along Via dei Musei, crossing Via Guisseppe Mazzini to Piazzetta Tito Speri. Beyond, a left enters Piazza Loggia, which leads back to the starting point.

what to see

Lago di Garda

While the Italians share Lakes Maggiore and Lugano geographically with the Swiss and Lake Como historically with the British, they share Lake Garda with the Germans and Austrians. In waterside restaurants and cafés, it's almost unusual to hear Italian spoken at neighbouring tables. Despite this influx of tourism from the north through the Brenner Pass, Garda retains its Italian character, especially on its western shore.

Vintage lake steamer poster

Mountains provide a backdrop for the northern end of Lake Garda

what to see

The largest of Italy's lakes, Garda covers more than 350sq km (135sq miles), and is 83km (52 miles) long. Narrow at the northern end, where it is hemmed in by mountains, the lake widens to the south, with a shoreline of gently rolling hills. Its beauty has inspired writers since Goethe's time (German tourists are not a new phenomenon) and perhaps D H Lawrence, who lived in Gargnano, described the lake most lyrically in *Twilight in Italy*.

This lake, like the others to the west, enjoys a mild year-round climate, so the vegetation that surrounds it – palms, olives and lemons – grows further north than is usual. The road that encircles the lake is the most scenic in the mountainous north, but spends a lot of time in tunnels along the western shore. If circling the lake, the scenery is best when driven in an anti-clockwise direction, travelling north along the east side and south on the west. Traffic is heaviest on the southern part of the lake.

Every town of any size is connected to the others by boats which circle the lake, and shorter shuttles are provided between nearby towns. Southern towns have more options; in the north there may well be a long wait for the next boat circling the lake.
Navigazione Lago di Garda. Tel: (030) 914 9511. www.navigazionelaghi.it. Operates: June–mid Sept.

Limone sul Garda has a tiny enclosed harbour

THE LIMONI RIVIERA

No one claims that Garda's northwestern shore is undiscovered, and cafés and boutiques are plentiful along the narrow lanes of candy-coloured houses, covered with bougainvillea. Yet that does not diminish the charm of the easy lakeside promenades of its towns. Connected by SS-45, which spends more time in tunnels than revealing lake views, these towns are worth exploring.

Gardone Riviera

If Gardone seems to lack cohesion, blame its geography. The narrow space between the water and the road, coupled with the enormous garden that is the town's steeply sloping centrepiece, makes it hard to fit in much else. The result is two towns, one a promenade of well-dressed, Belle Epoque hotels and villas along the shore, and the other the hill top **Gardone di Sopra**, whose picturesque square faces **Il Vittoriale** (see pp116–17). Between lies **Giardino Botanico Hruska**, 10,000m^2 (107,600sq ft) of botanical gardens. Cascading in terraces of exotic trees, plants from every continent thrive around pools, fountains and

sculpture in the mild lake climate.
Via Roma. Open: daily Mar–Oct during daylight hours.

A public park surrounds **Villa Alba**, built as the summer estate of a German Kaiser. **Torre San Marco**, the stone tower of its dock, is a landmark on the shore below. Gardone's promenade is a pleasant place to while away the early evening.
ARPT (tourist information centre), Corso Republica 8. Tel: (0365) 203 47. www.info-gardone.it

Limone sul Garda

Protected by the knife-sharp stone ridges behind it, Limone long ago turned its sheltered slope into terraced lemon groves. Tourism has largely replaced lemons, but some still grow along the shore and above the town's winding lanes of pastel-coloured stucco buildings. A large car park at the information kiosk on SS-45 handles the overflow when the more convenient one at the end of Lungolago Marconi, the long lakefront promenade, is full. Shopping, cafés and strolling past the little Porto Vecchio is what Limone is all about. A car ferry connects to Malcesine from the south end of the Lungolago Marconi.
ARPT (tourist information centre), Via IV Novembre (SS45). Tel: (0365) 918 987. www.info-limone.it

Salo

Sitting at the end of a long bay, Salo is the largest town on the eastern shore. Its claim to historic fame is as the site of Mussolini's puppet republic in the final years of World War II. The **Duomo** has a splendid gilded wooden altarpiece and choirs, as well as a wealth of Renaissance paintings, including several by Romanino. Unfortunately, it is so poorly lighted that the paintings are all but impossible to see. The Renaissance portal is all the more noticeable because it stands in a still unfinished facade.
Vicolo Campanili. Tel: (0365) 521 700. Open: Daily 9am–noon & 3.30–6.30pm. ARPT (tourist information centre), Via Lungolago Zanardelli 52. Tel: (0365) 214 23. www.info-salo.it. Open: daily in summer.

Toscolano-Maderno

The highlight of these twinned villages is the 12th-century Romanesque church of **Sant'Andrea** with a crypt beneath the sanctuary, and good remnants of its original frescoes in the crypt, over the pulpit and in the aisle vaulting. The most outstanding feature, however, is the intricate stone carving on the pillars of the nave and surrounding the portal – animals and highly complicated knot patterns are the best of these.
Pza San Marco. Open: daily 9am–noon & 3–6pm.

Altar of Salo's Duomo

Il Vittoriale

For the last years of his life, the highly gifted poet and writer, Gabriele d'Annunzio, devoted his attention to his villa high above Lake Garda – Il Vittoriale. There, with his friend the architect Gian Carlo Maroni, d'Annunzio created an art deco never-never land to house his collections and indulge his decorating whims. If in the process he created a monument to himself, he at least assured that he and his work would be remembered.

Il Vittoriale is not easy to forget. The interior is open only with a guided tour, necessary to navigate the maze of connecting rooms and passageways, and to find the truly significant pieces amid the jumble. The tour tells something of the poet's life and exploits of derring-do, to put the artefacts in perspective.

The music room is draped in black – even the ceilings, where the drapes and a large snakeskin are suspended on gold cord. The few lights are muted by glass shades. The dark was not altogether a product of d'Annunzio's gloomy psyche. He had lost an eye in a World War I flying accident – he was a decorated pilot – and the remaining eye was left photophobic, making dark far more comfortable for him.

A veranda off the bedroom – stuffed with china knick-knacks and heaped with dozens of silk pillows – contains a rare glimpse of personal items: a photo of d'Annunzio's mother and of his earlier love, actress Eleanora Duse. An unexplained Little Red Riding Hood doll sits in a birdbath. Some 900 objects decorate one bathroom, in which the dark blue, art deco bathtub matches the sink and bidet.

Perhaps the most curious room contains a coffin, where d'Annunzio lay to contemplate the meaning of death; here his body lay for a night of vigil after his death. He died in the small study at his desk, aged 75. His work, long shunned due to his Fascist associations, is back in fashion. He had written speeches for Mussolini in the early days, but later became more critical, fuelling Il Duce's worst fears and sealing d'Annunzio's virtual house arrest here.

Mussolini feared that this charismatic war hero who had once stirred the patriotic emotions of the Italian people with his words and his audacious feats (he once flew a squadron over Vienna to drop inflammatory pamphlets) might do so again, and not to Il Duce's benefit. Thus, he showered d'Annunzio with laurels, named him president of the Italian Royal Academy, proclaimed his villa a national monument, and made sure he stayed there.

Il Vittoriale sits in a hillside park, on whose gardens d'Annunzio lavished as much unrestrained largess as he gave the house. A ship is imbedded into the hillside as a memorial to two comrades who died in the private invasion of Fiume (where d'Annunzio and his followers set up a government of their own). Above, his almost absurd mausoleum rises, like a marble wedding cake, tier upon tier to a surmounting plinth on which rests his tomb.

Il Vittoriale degli Italiani, *Via Vittoriale, Gardone di Sopra. Tel: (0365) 201 30. Grounds open: daily Apr–Sept 8.30am–8pm, Oct–Mar 9am–5pm. House open: daily Apr–Sept 9.30am–7pm, Oct–Mar Tue–Sun 9am–1pm & 2–5pm. Admission charge.*

Opposite: Il Vittoriale is designed in Art Deco style
Above: A ship is embedded in the hillside garden
Below: d'Annunzio's tomb surmounts a gigantic mausoleum

THE NORTHEAST SHORE AND MONTE BALDO

Two castles, one set majestically on a high point above the lake, alpine scenery and lovely little harbours of bright boats give variety to the northeastern shore. This is where Lake Garda suddenly narrows to the mountain-bound terrain common to the other lakes. The resulting wind currents make the shore popular with sailors and windsurfers, while the long ridge of Monte Baldo attracts walkers.

Brenzone

Dotting the lakeshore with its colourful little villages, Brenzone's prettiest spot is hidden from S-249, but the little river that cascades past the road marks its location. Park in the tiny *piazza* south of the cascade and walk beside the river to the charming little port. Here, a bridge arches across the stream which opens into a little harbour surrounded by brightly-coloured houses. A round stone tower guards the far side, punctuating one of the lake's most photogenic ensembles.

Malcesine

On a rounded peninsula, backed by Monte Baldo and faced across the lake by some of the most rugged and beautiful shoreline, Malcesine is a match for its setting. Cobbled medieval streets wind upwards, past art studios and small shops to **Castello Scaligero**, which perches on a cliff high above the lake. In the 1870s, German poet Goethe was arrested as a spy for drawing a picture of it, but photographers and artists are safe there today. Castles don't get better

Sampling olive oils

surroundings, and beaches don't get any better views than that of the tiny cove at its foot, reached by steep steps from Via Posterna. Inside the castle, a museum displays some of Goethe's drawings.
Tel: (045) 657 0333. Open: daily mid Mar–Oct 9am–8pm (last admittance 7.30pm), Dec–mid Jan 10am–5pm, mid Jan–mid Mar Sat–Sun only. Admission charge. Closed Nov.

There is a covered car park on the hillside above S-249, and a car ferry crosses the lake from Malcesine to Limone sul Garda.
ARPT (tourist information centre), Via Capitanato 6. Tel: (045) 740 0040/ (045) 740 0837. www.malcesinepiu.it www.aptgardaveneto.com

Monte Baldo

Views of the lake and to the pre-Alp and Dolomite peaks are a ten-minute ride from Malcesine. A modern 360-degree, windowed *funivia* (cable car) carries passengers up Monte Baldo to 1,650m (5,400ft) for panoramas and access to the walking trails along the ridge. Monte Baldo is known for its abundance of alpine wild flowers. In winter, the *funivia* becomes a ski lift leading to smaller lifts that reach 11km (6.8 miles) of upper snowfields.
Funicolari Malcesine–Monte Baldo.
Tel: (045) 740 0206. Operates: daily Apr–Oct 8am–5pm, June–mid Sept until 7pm.

Torri del Benaco

The 14th-century **Castello Scaligero**, built (as most castles in this region) by Verona's della Scala family, overlooks a little marina. Its small museum concentrates on local crafts.
Tel: (045) 629 6111. Open: daily June–Sept 9.30am–1pm & 4.30–7.30pm, Apr–May, Oct 9.30am–12.30pm & 2.30–6pm. Admission charge.

A ferry carries cars across the midpoint of the lake to Gardone Riviera.
Tourist Information, Viale Lavanda.
Tel: (045) 722 5120. Open: daily June–Aug 8.35am–7.45pm.

Malcesine sits on a peninsula, crowned by a castle

THE OLIVI RIVIERA

Olive groves, growing far north of their usual range, give the gentle hills here a soft green colour, and their name – the olive shore. Although this is the most heavily visited part of the lake, the Riviera's former fishing towns are attractive and well-kept – which is why so many people come here.

Bardolino

Bardolino's shaded benches invite visitors to enjoy the view of the lake front. A cycling and walking path follows the lake shore from Bardolino to Torre del Benaco, and passes the car park just north of the town. Most streets between S-249 and the promenade are closed to all traffic.
Tourist Information Centre, *Piazzale Aldo Moro. Tel: (045) 721 0078. www.info-bardolino.it*

Two early churches are close to the main road. The 9th-century Carolingian

Marina at Lazise

The church of San Severo

San Zeno, although well-signposted is rarely open, but the 11th-century Romanesque **San Severo** usually is. Easy to spot by its tall, cone-topped tower, San Severo preserves many original frescoes and some excellent early stone carving on the capitals. The crypt below the altar (be careful of the well-worn steps) has intricate knot designs carved in its posts.

The region's olive groves give rise to a major local olive oil industry, explored in **Museo dell'Olio d'Oliva** on S-249 just south of the town (and difficult to enter and exit by car). Here you can compare flavours, buy olive products, and tour the excellent displays. Early presses and containers illustrate the origins of olive oil, and visitors learn that the tree is not native to Italy but was spread around the Mediterranean by Romans.
Via Peschiera 54 (S-249), Cisano di Bardolino. Tel: (045) 622 9024. Open: Mon–Sat 9am–12.30pm & 3–7pm, Sun & Holidays 9am–12.30pm. Free admission.

Bardolino is best known for its red wine which has its own interesting, although less ambitious, **Museo del**

Romanesque frescoes cover San Zeno's interior

Vino at the Zeni winery. English signage describes winemaking methods, and artefacts include presses and tools from the 1800s, and Roman and Etruscan *amphorae*. Summer wine tasting evenings need to be pre-booked.
Via Costabella 9. Tel: (045) 622 8331. www.museodelvino.it. Open: mid Mar–Oct Mon–Fri 9am–1pm & 2–7pm, Sat–Sun 9am–1pm & 2–6pm. Free admission, charge for tastings.

Garda

Garda is purely for pleasure, a place to sit in a café or on a lakeside bench and enjoy the view. Or, for the more active, walk or cycle along the shore path to **San Vigilio**, a scenic point with a pebble beach and beautiful views past a 16th-century *palazzo* and tall cypresses.
ARPT (tourist information centre), Via Don Gnocchi 25. Tel: (045) 627 0384. www.aptgardaveneto.com

Lazise

A tidy marina of bright boats sits alongside an arcaded Venetian customs house and a 12th-century stone church, **San Nicolo**, interesting for its frescoes. The inevitable Scaligeri castle, from the 11th century, is not open to visit.
ARPT (tourist information centre), Via Fontana 14. Tel: (045) 758 0114. www.info-lazise.it

Orto Botanica del Monte Baldo

Specimens of Monte Baldo's abundant indigenous alpine plants, including edelweiss and alpine lilies, thrive in these botanic gardens, reached by following the signposted road from Garda to Caprino Veronese. At Spiazzi, the sanctuary of **Madonna della Corona** overlooks the Adige valley to the east.
Ferrara di Monte Baldo. Tel: (045) 624 7065. Open: daily May–mid Sept 9am–6pm.

RIVA AND THE GARDATRENTINO

The River Sarco flows into Lake Garda from between two mountain ranges which protect the river's valley from Alpine cold. Since prehistoric times, this mild climate has attracted settlement, and its many castles attest to the valley's importance as a trading route.
ARPT (tourist information centre), Giardina di Porta Orientale 8, Riva del Garda. Tel: (0464) 554 444.
www.gardatrentino.it

Arco

Curling around a shaft of vertical cliffs, Arco's old town centre would be a pleasant place to wander even without its castle. On top of the cliffs stands **Castello d'Arco** with a room of 14th-century frescoes that illustrate Medieval court games and chivalry. Stairs and a path climb the slightly gentler western slope.
Tel: (0464) 510 156. Open: daily Apr–Sept 10am–7pm, Oct–Mar 10am–4pm (Fresco room closes one hour earlier).

Also on the western side of town, **Arco Arboreto** contains exotic trees which flourish in the valley's unusually mild micro-climate.
Via Lomego. Open: daily Apr–Sept 8am–7pm, Oct–Mar 9am–4pm.

Hotel Europa overlooks the boat landing at Riva

Castello Drena

Hanging above the Salagoni Gorge, the walls and tall single tower of Drena date back to the 1100s. Inside, a museum shows Bronze Age archaeological finds from the valley.
Tel: (0464) 541 220. Open: Apr–Oct Tue–Sun 10am–6pm, Nov–Mar Sat–Sun 10am–6pm. Admission charge.

Ceniga

North of Arco, the River Sarca is spanned by a Roman bridge, **Ponte Romana**. Beside it a little picnic area is shaded by olive trees. Bordering the narrow lane, an amazing assortment of fruits grow – kiwi, bananas and figs, along with the expected grapes. **Sentiro de Marocce**, a mountain hiking trail, begins at the bridge.

Riva del Garda

Monte Brione rises precipitously from Riva's old town, which crowds between the cliff and lake. At its heart, Piazza 3 Novembre is surrounded by café-filled colonnades and the 13th-century Torre Aponale (Clock Tower) that chimes the hour. The *piazza* opens on to the lake at the passenger boat landing. A shore promenade leads past parks and glorious formal gardens to the nearby town of **Torbole**, the windsurfing capital of the lake.

The castle **Rocca di Riva** sits on a little island formed by its own moat. It houses an excellent museum on the prehistoric settlements here that has unusual Copper Age steli, and a collection of Medieval armour. ***Museo Civico**, Piazza Cesare Battista. Tel: (0464) 573 869. Open: Sept–June Tue–Sun 9am–5.30pm, daily July–Aug 9am–5.30pm. Admission charge.*

A pleasant all-day excursion on the lake is offered on the sailing ship *Siora Veronica*, which sails (*daily, 8.30am*) from the castle moat's inlet.
Tel: (0335) 548 3030. www.letsgosailing.it

Plunging from a lake through a 100m (328ft) deep vertical hole in the rock, **Cascata de Varone** is possibly Italy's most dramatic waterfall. English signs explain how the water's force carved the corkscrew-shaped tunnel, creating an ecosystem so cool and wet that it has its own flora.
Tel: (0464) 521 421. Open: daily May–Aug 9am–7pm, daily Apr, Sept 9am–6pm, daily Mar, Oct 10am–12.30pm & 2–5pm, Nov–Feb Sun 10am–12.30pm & 2–5pm.

Arco's castle stands above the town centre

SOUTHERN GARDA

Some of the busiest lake towns are on its southern shore, but here also is the lake's prize town, Sirmione.

The Valtenesi – the hilly region between the lake and the valley of the Chiese River to the west – is a land of farms, vineyards and olive groves, its scenery often bordered by ridge lines of dark cypress trees. This is just the antidote for the busy roads and beaches of the southern shore.

The best beach along the Valtenesi shore is south of Manerba (follow signs to the *spaggia* (beach)). A long beach with more facilities, but also more people and less atmosphere, is at Lido di Lonato, where there are tent pitches.

Castle towns of the Valtenesi

Castles seem to crown every high point along the lake's shore and into the hills that rise behind it. However, from below the passing traveller cannot see that some of these contain whole villages snugly encased inside the walls.
Tourist Co-op Valtenesi, Via Risorgimento 5, Manerba del Garda. Tel: (0365) 626 41. www.gardavaltenesi.com

Inside the square castle at **Moniga**, starched rows of brightly painted houses line the outer walls to form a tiny city. A larger fortress, surrounded by olive groves, tops the hill at **Padenghi sul Garda**, reached by Via Castello. From the summit there are views across the lake, and hidden inside is an entire town of stone houses, their backyard vegetable gardens tucked against the warm stones of its wall. The castle is large enough for the town to have three long parallel streets and a full-grown pomegranate tree in one garden. The fortress was begun in the 10th century, but the present walls are from the 14th century.

Amid the rolling vineyards of the Valtenese hills, to the west of Lake Garda, no town hides inside the walls of the castle at **Soiano del Lago**. Its courtyard is used for concerts in the summer, and a nature park starts at the long alley of cypress trees that leads from its gate.

Desenzano del Garda

Conveniently located at the base of the lake, and the lake's only town with a train station, Desenzano makes an ideal base, especially for those using public transport. The A-4 *autostrada* (motorway) is also close. Shops and restaurants surround the pretty marina, and castle ruins top the town's low hill. An excavated Roman villa, **Villa Romana**, has some excellent mosaics.
Via Scavi Romani. Tel: (030) 914 3547. Open: Sat 9.30am–12.30pm & 2.30–5.30pm. Admission charge.

Look into the parish church of **Santa Maria Maddalena** to see the painting, *Last Supper*, by Tiepolo. **Museo Archeologico Rambotti** has Roman artefacts and those from earlier peoples.
Viale Tomasa dal Molin. Tel: (030) 914 4529. Open Tue–Sat 9.30am–12.30pm & 2.30–5.30pm. Admission charge.

Tuesday is not a good day to drive into Desenzano, since the weekly market covers the entire waterfront with stalls selling everything from Valtenesi farm cheeses to jewellery.
ARPT (tourist information centre), Porta Vecchia. Tel: (030) 914 1510. www.info-desenzano.it

Sirmione's picture-perfect castle is surrounded by a moat

Peschiera

Since the Romans first settled at Lake Garda, everyone has had a hand in fortifying Peschiera, which is where the River Mincio flows from the lake.

The last were the Austrians, who in the mid-19th century beefed up the walls the Venetians had built in order to protect Peschiera from Italians set on independence. A century later,

what to see

Gelati in every conceivable flavour tempts visitors to Sirmione the Germans moved in, using the charming old *palazzo* as their command headquarters during World War II.

La Rocca, the 2,300m (7,550ft) of fortifications, surrounds the old port with grass-topped walls which form a bridge at the end of the colourful marina. Arriving from the A-4 motorway, bear left through the main gate, **Porta Verona**.
Complesso Monumentale. Open: daily 9am–12.30pm & 2.30–6pm. Admission charge.

There is a car park on the lake front at the port, opposite the ARPT tourist information office.
Piazzale Bettoni 15. Tel: (045) 755 1673. www.info-peschiera.it. Open: Mar–Oct Mon–Sat 8am–1pm & 3–6pm, Sun 8am–1pm. Closed Sun–Mon and pm during winter.

Sirmione

The Romans were the first to take their holidays at the tip of the 3km (2 miles) long tongue of land that juts into the centre of the lake. Built in the 1st century, Grotte de Catullo was an exceptionally large villa in an exceptionally beautiful location. Surrounded by olive trees at the very tip of the peninsula, it includes the ruins of arches, a hall, a swimming pool and a corridor overlooking the lake. The museum houses the archaeological finds.
Tel: (030) 916 157. Open Tue–Sun 9am–dusk. Admission charge.

A dozen centuries later, the della Scala family of Verona defended the entrance to the town with a castle, **Rocca Scaligeri**, still in excellent condition. The moat around the castle makes an island of the town. Inside the double row of defensive walls there is a museum of Roman and Medieval archaeological finds, but the main attraction of the castle's interior is the view at the top. A harbour inside the castle's outer walls provided safe refuge for village fishing boats and the Scaligeri fleet.
Tel: (030) 916 468. Open: Apr–Oct Tue–Sun 8.30am–7.30pm, Nov–Mar Tue–Sun 9am–4pm. Admission charge.

Between the castle and the Roman villa is a town filled with designer shops and *gelati* (ice cream) bars. Among all this hides a trio of churches, the oldest of which is the 8th-century **San Pietro**, with 12th-century frescoes.
ARPT (tourist information centre), Viale Marconi. Tel: (030) 916 114. www.info-sirmione.it. Open: daily Apr–Oct 9am–12.30pm & 3–6pm, Nov–Mar Mon–Fri 9am–12.30pm & 3–6pm.

SCALIGERI CASTLES

You may notice in Northern Italy, especially in the region once controlled by the powerful della Scala family of Verona, notched crenulations on top of castle walls. This 'fishtail' shape is typical of a Medieval political group called the Ghibellines, supporters of the old feudal aristocracy and the emperor. Opposing them were the Guelphs, the rising middle class who supported the Pope in the constant tug-of-war between church and temporal power. Whenever you see these notched crenulations, you can be sure the builders were Ghibellines, and around Lake Garda most likely Scaligeri.

what to see

Driving Tour: Lake Idro Route

A scenic circular tour from Salo reaches two lakes that are seldom visited by tourists. The steep mountain sides vary from wooded to almost vertical cliffs falling on either side. A few sections of steep, winding road are not for those with vertigo, but the route is well maintained and the scenery unparalleled. A long tunnel bypasses the steepest portion. The most frustrating thing about this trip will be the scarcity of lay-bys from which to take photographs.
Allow 1–2 days.

Begin south of Salo from S-45b, following brown signposts along the Chiese River to 'Val Sabbio'.

1 Lago d'Idro
The first views of this long, narrow lake are above the town of Idro, at its southern end. An attractive picnic site with a children's playground overlooks the lake beside the road. Ahead, the northern end of the lake disappears into a series of steeply sloping mountain sides. At an altitude of 370m (1,214ft), Idro is the highest Lombardy lake.

2 Anfo
Plenty of tourist facilities, including an *albergo* (hotel), tent pitches and water sports centres, line the lake, overseen by the stone and stucco buildings of the upper older town, in whose castle Garibaldi made his headquarters.

3 Lodrone
The twin towns of Ponte Caffaro and Lodrone mark the boundary between

Lombardy and the Trentino, where the architecture begins to show Alpine influences almost immediately. Over the bridge, a winding road (on the right) leads to Troti-coltura Armanni, a trout and salmon farm. You can buy smoked fish, or just visit the rearing pools.
*Open: Mon–Fri 8am–noon & 1.30–5.30pm, Sat 8am–noon.
Shortly after Darzo, turn right, following signs to Riva or Riva del Garda.*

4 Storo
The old town clusters under a sheer cliff as the road winds past a rare public laundry basin, still in use. The road climbs quickly along a corniche before entering a narrow cleft which it shares with a rocky river. Watch out for a waterfall on the left, and a lay-by above on the left has a trail leading to the falls.

5 Passa Ampola
At 747m (2,450ft) altitude, the road enters a long green valley. A boardwalk provides access to the bird-rich, reedy, bio-reserve at Lago d'Ampola, called Biotopo. Rare lilies and aquatic plants grow in the reserve. At Tiarno di Sopra, just off the road to the left, brightly coloured houses enclosed by stone walls with flower boxes, line the river bank.

6 Lago di Ladro
Tiny Lago di Ladro is overlooked by woody mini-parks with benches. In attractive Molina di Ledro, **Museo delle Palafitte** displays Bronze Age artefacts from archaeological excavations dating back to the second millennium BC. One of the dwellings has been reconstructed.
Tel: (0464) 508 182. Open: mid June–mid Sept 10am–1pm & 2–6pm, mid Sept–mid June 9am–1pm & 2–5pm. Admission charge.

7 Pre
The steep road descending from Molina di Ladro looks directly down on to the rooftops of Pre, whose hillsides are green with farms and vineyards. Pre is at the bottom of a valley so steep that from November to February its residents see neither sun nor moon.
A long tunnel leads almost directly into Riva del Garda, and S-45b, which follows the lake shore back to Salo.

Tiny mountain towns overlook Lake Idro

Excursion: Rovereto

Less than 25km (15 miles) from the northern end of Lake Garda, Rovereto is a city packed with history. Dinosaurs lived here and left their footprints in mud that solidified to rock, preserving the prints intact. Jump ahead to the 20th century, and this area witnessed some of the bitterest World War I campaigns. In between these times, castles were built, churches decorated, vineyards planted, and the results of this all combine to make Rovereto and its environs a fascinating destination.

ARPT (tourist information centre), Via Dante 63.
Tel: (0464) 430 363. www.apt.rovereto.tn.it

Rooftops of Rovereto

Castello de Rovereto

Crowning the city, this 13th-century fortress looks over the red-roofed town to steep mountains that enclose the Adige valley. The museum gives a dramatic and poignant picture of the impact that World War I had on all of Northern Italy. The artefacts, photographs and posters are so graphic and well-arranged that the story is clear in any language. Look through the racks of photographs showing the liberation of towns and compare nearby Riva del Garda then and now.

Via Castello. Open: July–Sept Tue–Sun 8.30am–6.30pm, mid Mar–June, Oct–Nov Tue–Sun 9am–12.30pm & 2–6pm.

Dinosaur tracks

Spread over the mountain side, south of town, are about 350 footprints of prehistoric creatures, dating back 200 million years. Along with distinct single foot imprints, there are entire paths of dinosaur tracks. The first of these is a 15-minute walk from the road, and the tracks continue for some distance. Well-illustrated signs help to interpret the tracks and the animals that left them.

Follow signs for the Ossario di Castel Dante, then follow Strada degli Artiglieri to the car park, clearly marked.

Strada degli Artiglieri

After seeing pictures in the castle museum, the memorials lining the road to the dinosaur tracks – and the name of the road itself – fall into place. In World War I, Italian soldiers dragged and pushed heavy artillery up this steep route, digging defensive positions into the mountain side. The memorials are to men lost here. Each evening Rovereto commemorates the thousands who died by ringing the huge bell named the **Maria Dolens**, cast from cannons contributed by both sides that fought in the war.

Villa Lagarina

Across the Adige, this tiny village calls itself the 'Little Saltzburg', and there is a connection. The church of **Santa Maria Assunta** was created by the same artists that built Saltzburg's cathedral. Their style is clear in the marble altar and elaborate baroque stucco work. Although such baroque interiors are common to the north, this is one of the few so far south.
Open: Mon–Sat 9am–1pm & 3–5pm, Sun during service.

Vini Vallagarina

Wineries are dotted around the valley surrounding Rovereto, and there is an association of wineries that welcomes visitors to the tastings of a number of local varieties. All the wines there are for sale.
Via Brancolino 4, Nogaredo. Tel: (0464) 412 073. Open: Mon–Fri 8am–noon & 2–6pm.

Rovereto's impressive castle contains a museum of the World Wars

what to see

Verona

In few cities do the Roman, Medieval and Renaissance remain so distinct, yet blend so harmoniously as they do in this lovely city tucked into a sweeping 'S' curve of the Adige River.

'Juliet's Balcony' was actually added in the 1930s

Today's city centre, the heart of life for the Veronese, is exactly where it was when the Romans walked its streets. The pedestrianised area includes the old forum (parts of which are visible) and one of Italy's most charming, enclosed Medieval/Renaissance squares, Piazza dei Signori. More Medieval and Renaissance buildings line the streets, which pass through Roman and Medieval gates to reach a castellated bridge and the well-preserved Medieval Castelvecchio on the river. Reminders that this town was the pride of the Venetian empire are found in the gracefully arched windows and the winged lion of St Mark, perched on a column surveying Piazza delle Erbe's morning market.

The area is easily explored on foot since most attractions are clustered together in the old city's walking streets. Via Mazzini connects Piazza Bra and the Roman arena to Piazza Erbe and, in the other direction, Via Roma leads to Castelvecchio and the river.

Verona is on the main Milan–Venice train line, and just north of the A-4 *autostrada*. Catullo Airport is in Villafranca, about 10km (6 miles) southwest, en route to Mantova. Shuttles run every 20 minutes between the airport and the railway station at Porta Nova. *Tel: (045) 805–7911. Operates: 6am–11.30pm.*

Although most central streets are closed to traffic, hotel guests may enter to unload luggage. Metered parking can be found along the river on Lungoadige Capuleti, near Ponte Aleardi bridge. A 24-hour car park is just south of Piazza Bra, at Piazza Cittadella. Some hotels have spaces reserved for clients. To use a bus, buy a ticket before boarding from a news-stand or tobacco shop. Inexpensive daily tourist tickets are available and a VeronaCard (buy at news-stands or participating attractions) combines museum admissions with bus transport. Taxi ranks are at Piazza Bra, Porto Nuovo (railway station), Piazza Erbe and Piazza San Zeno; cabs are metered. Radio-dispatched taxis: *Tel: (045) 532 666. ARPT (helpful for lodging recommendations), Via Alpini 9, off Piazza Bra. Tel: (045) 806 8680. Fax: (045) 800 3638.*

The *tourist information office* is adjacent to a complex of travel facilities including a café, lockers and public conveniences. *Ponte Aleardi at Via Pallone and Via Macello. Open Mon–Fri 9am–6pm, Sat–Sun 9am–12.30pm & 2–5.30pm.*

Via Mazzini connects Piazza Bra and Piazza Erbe

WHEREFORE ART THOU, JULIET?

Luigi da Porto, a writer from Vicenza, borrowed the names of two local families when he wrote the original version of *Romeo and Juliet*, but it was William Shakespeare who made audiences take the characters to heart. In fact, they – or at least Juliet – take on a life of their own as Verona's number one tourist attraction. The entirely fictional story is set in Verona, and the city at first humoured tourists by assigning Juliet a Medieval 'home' and even adding an appropriate balcony in the 1930s. A more recent addition is a tomb for the heroine. Romeo is largely ignored, although a fine Medieval house opposite the della Scala tombs has been assigned to him.

Casa di Giulietta is always filled with tourists

L'Arena di Verona

For almost two millennia, the arena has been a focal point in Verona. Since AD 30 it has served as a field for gladiators, a place of refuge from barbarian invasions and, from 1913, the venue for one of Europe's foremost opera festivals, the Stagione Lirico di Verona. With a seating capacity of about 22,000, Verona's arena is the third largest and best preserved in Italy, with only a portion of its outer ring missing. The arena forms one side of **Piazza Bra**, social centre of the Veronese. A phalanx of cafés in a row of 19th-century buildings forms another side of the *piazza*, and the 14th-century **Palazzo della Gran Guardia** adjoins the arched **Portone della Bra** gate on the south side. This is where the Veronese begin their evening stroll, walking past the busy cafés and along fashionable Via Mazzini. *Piazza Bra. Open: daily 8am–7pm, on opera days 8.15am–3.30pm. Admission charge.*

Casa di Giulietta

Through the efforts of a few romantics and, we suspect, many promoters, a fine medieval building with a balcony (added in the 1930s) came to be the 'home' of fictional Juliet from *Romeo and Juliet*, and is now a mecca for hoards of tourists. The walls leading into the small courtyard have literally been covered with graffiti, and the breast of the bronze

statue of the charming heroine is burnished from the touching of thousands of hands.
Via Cappello 23. Tel: (045) 803 4303. Open: Tue–Sun 8.30am–7.30pm, Mon 1.30–7.30pm. Free admission to courtyard, charge to enter house.

Castelvecchio and Ponte Scaligero

Cangrande II built this impressive brick castle along the River Adige between 1355 and 1375 to secure his family's rule over the city. He connected it to the opposite bank with the **Ponte Scaligero**, castellated to make the bridge defensible. The castle, later an officers' mess for the Italian army, today houses one of Italy's premier art museums, with works by Bellini, Pisano, Francheschi, Rubens, Falconetti, Montagna, Tintoretto, Tiepolo and Guardi. Walking from room to room takes you through a history of Italian secular and religious art from the 13th through to the 19th centuries, with most artefacts originating from palaces, churches and monasteries in Verona and its province.

Corso Castelvecchio (end of Corso Cavour). Tel: (045) 594 734. Open: Tue–Sun 8.30am–7.30pm, Mon 1.30–7.30pm, last entry 6pm. Admission charge.

Duomo di Santa Maria Matricolare

Verona's cathedral is a fine example of the blending of architectural styles. On the site of a Roman temple and later a 5th-century Christian church, the present church was begun in 1139. In the centuries it took to complete, Romanesque, Gothic and Renaissance styles of architecture washed over Italy and were incorporated in the cathedral. The two-storey Romanesque portal is by medieval sculptor Nicolo, and Titian's 1530 painting of the Assumption is located in the first chapel to the left. The choir screen is the work of Michele Sanmicheli (1484–1559) who designed many of Verona's palaces and reworked the city defences.
Pza Duomo. Tel: (045) 592 813. Open: Mon–Sat 9.30am–6pm, Sun 1.30–6pm.

Cafés on Piazza Bra

Giardino Giusti

Nestled into the steep-sided hills of the city on the east side of the River Adige, the Giusti Gardens provide a cool place to walk, rest or picnic. Designed and built during the 15th and 16th centuries, they are a fine example of Renaissance landscape architecture. Formal parterres of clipped hedges, walkways, cypress trees and grottos occupy the lower level, and stepped pathways lead upwards to views over the garden.
Via Giardini Giusti 2.
Tel: (045) 803 4029. Open: daily Apr–Sept 9am–8pm, Oct–Mar 9am–7pm.

Palazzo de Ragione and Lamberti Tower

The 84m (275ft) Lamberti Tower rises above the east side of Piazza delle Erbe, easily identified by its striped layers of pink brick and white tufa. It is part of the Medieval Palazzo de Ragione which has served as law courts for centuries. Walk through the archway and around into its courtyard for a view of the Renaissance stairway that leads to the upper levels. The tower, with splendid views of the Dolomites on clear days, is accessible by lift or stairs.
Pza dei Signori. Open: Sun–Sat 9.30am–7.30pm, Mon 1.30–7.30pm. Admission charge for the lift.

Piazza delle Erbe

The long narrow shape of Piazza delle Erbe hints at its one-time role as the Roman Hippodrome. Medieval buildings, some with fine frescoes on their outer walls, line its edges. Almost from the beginning, this space has served as an important marketplace.

Scaligeri Tombs

The Roman statue in the centre, the **Madonna of Verona**, acquired this role only in 1368. The Lion of Saint Mark, on its column at one end, was erected during Venetian rule and the **Palazzo Mafei** just behind it dates from the 17th century. Excavated remnants of the Roman temple of Jupiter are visible inside.

Piazza dei Signori

One of the loveliest in the city, this piazza is surrounded by the palaces of Verona's Medieval rulers, the della Scala family. In the centre is an 1865 statue of Dante Alighiere who took refuge in Verona during his exile from Florence. Along one side of the *piazza* is the **Loggia del Consiglia** with frescoes and statues of local notables. Look on the palace wall for the denunciation box where Medieval Veronese could get rid

what to see

of a rival by dropping a discreet note to the Duke.

San Fermo Maggiore

In the 11th century, the old church became the crypt of the Benedictines' new church. It changed again in 1260 when the Franciscans added the Gothic pink brick and white tufa facade, but throughout all the renovations, the crypt remained little changed, retaining 7th- and 8th-century frescoes. The marble pulpit dates from 1396, the work of Antonio da Mestre.
Stradone San Fermo. Tel: (045) 592 813. Open: Mon–Sat 10am–6pm, Sun 1–6pm.

Scaligeri tombs

Adjoining Piazza dei Signori, the small elegant church of **Santa Marie Antica**, consecrated in 1185, was the family church of the della Scala family and it was here that they were laid to rest. The two tombs with mounted warriors are of Cansignorio (who died in 1375) and Mastino II who died in 1351. The former was designed by Bonino da Campione and the latter was sculpted by Giovanni di Rigino.
Via Arche Scaligeri, off Pza dei Signori. Open: tombs always visible. Church open: daily 7.30am–12.30pm & 3–7pm. Admission charge.

Modern bronze panels on the doors of San Fermo Maggiore

Courtyard of Tomba di Giulietta

San Zeno Major
Named for the first Bishop of Verona, and last rebuilt between 1123–35, San Zeno is considered one of Europe's finest examples of Romanesque architecture. The 12-section rose window, attributed to Brioloto, dates from the 8th century. The portico columns resting on the backs of lions are believed to be by Nicolo. The triumph of Medieval artistry in a church replete with it, may be the 11th- and 12th-century bronze panels on the front doors. The left panels, the oldest, depict the life of Christ. On the right there are old testament events and two miracles of San Zeno, whose remains rest in the glass-enclosed coffin in the crypt. The wooden, polychromed ceiling of the nave dates from 1386, and Andrea Mantegna's most celebrated triptych, painted in 1457, is on the main alter. The adjoining cloisters are Romanesque and Gothic.
Pza San Zeno. Tel: (045) 592 813. Open Mon–Sat 8.30am–6pm, Sun 1–6pm.

Sant'Anastasia
It took from 1290 until the 15th century to complete this church, and even then the facade was never finished. An attractive arched portico surrounds doors attributed to Piero da Porlezza. Just inside the entrance is a pair of very unusual holy water fonts, the one on the left is called *Gobbo* (Humpback) and was sculpted by Gabriele Caliari, father of artist Paulo Veronese, in 1495. Near the Pellegrini chapel is the restored fresco *Saint George and the Princess*, painted by Pisanello in 1438.
Pza Sant'Anastasia. Tel: (045) 592 813. Open: Mon–Sat 9am–6pm, Sun 1–6pm.

Roman Porta Borsari

Santa Maria in Organo
Built in the 15th century, this church contains outstanding inlaid wood marquetry, the work of Fra Giovanni da Verona in the late 1400s. Decorating the choir stalls, lectern and sacristy, the inlay simulates everyday things. Shelves of books and display cupboards are an illusion, as are the lifelike chickens and rabbits.
Pza Isolo Sorge, Via San Chiara.

Teatro Romano and Museo Archeologico
Still used today, the 1st-century BC Roman theatre has much of its original seating, but the performance areas are contemporary. Shakespeare plays are staged here, as well as classical music, jazz, ballet and other drama. The theatre overlooks the five-arch span of Ponte Pietra, a Roman bridge rebuilt after its destruction in World War II. Above the theatre seats is a small museum of Roman artefacts, especially stone-carved architectural details.
Regaste Redentore 2. Tel: (045) 800 0360. Open: Tue–Sun 8.30am–7.30pm, Mon 1.30–7.30pm. Closed: performance nights. Admission charge.

Scavi Archeologici and Roman Gates
The Scavi are the archaeological digs that have brought Verona's Roman past back into view. Look on Via Cappello, off Piazza delle Erbe, for part of the Roman Forum and a Roman city gate, **Porta Leoni**. The remains of the forum are below street level, ringed by a rail for easy viewing.

Tomba di Giulietta e Museo Degli Affreschi
Even fictional heroines must have tombs. This ancient stone sarcophagus is empty but atmospheric. It is in a former convent which has become a small museum of fresco art. Be prepared for more of the Romeo and Juliet cult excesses.
Via Shakespeare (off Via del Pontiere). Tel: (045) 800 0361. Open: Tue–Sun 8.30am–7.30pm, Mon 1.30–7.30pm. Admission charge.

Holy water font in Sant'Anastasia

Walk: Old Verona

With many of its prime sights so close, and connected by pedestrianised streets, the best way to see Verona is by walking. Cafés and restaurants are well placed, offering plenty of opportunity to rest en route.

Although the walk could easily take two days with stops to tour each attraction and the museum at Castelvecchio, the walking time is about 2 hours.

Begin at Piazza Bra.

1 Arena di Verona
A good vantage point for contemplating the arena is a café on the north side of Piazza Bra.
Follow Via Alpini east along the south side of Piazza Bra, turning left at Via Maffei, which becomes Stradone San Fermo.

2 San Fermo
The church is on the right.
Continue past the church, turning left on Via Leoni, which becomes Via Cappello (see p137).

Madonna di Verona

3 Roman Forum
Excavations in the street show the pavement of the forum, and on the left is a Roman gate, which was hidden for centuries after being incorporated into a building. Beyond, on the right, is the courtyard of the so-called **Casa di Giulietta**.

4 Piazza delle Erbe
Straight ahead, this ancient market square is usually filled with the umbrellas of venders selling snacks, souvenirs and fresh produce. Notice the frescoes on the buildings along the side. Above is the **Lamberti Tower**.
Follow the passageway under the Lamberti Tower.

5 Piazza della Signori
Opposite the statue of Dante is the entrance to the Palazzo de Ragione and the tower.
From Piazza della Signori go through the arch at the north end of the square.

6 Scaligeri Tombs and Santa Maria Antica
On your right, the church is off a tiny piazza.

Past the tombs turn left and continue to Corso Sant'Anastasia, taking it to the right.

7 Sant'Anastasia
As well as this church, a 15th-century palace faces on to the small piazza, now the Hotel Due Torre.

Leaving the church, cross the piazza and turn right on Via Massalongo, following it one block and turning right on Via Ponte Pietra. Follow it to a small square, bearing left to reach the bridge.

8 Ponte Pietra and Teatro Romano
There is a good view of the theatre from the bridge. In the theatre is the Museo Archeologico.

Retrace your route across the bridge and turn right into Pza Broilo and bearing left to reach the back of the Duomo.

9 Duomo
Behind the Duomo is the small 8th-century church of San Giovanni in Fonte.

Leaving the Duomo, walk straight ahead to Via San Giacomo, turning left and following it to Corso Sant'Anastasia. Turn right, returning to Piazza delle Erbe, where the street becomes Corso Porta Borsari.

10 Corso Porta Borsari
This was the main street of Roman Verona, and you will pass through the 1st-century Roman gate, **Porta Borsari**. Further on, the 1st-century Roman **Arco dei Gavi**, along the river, was moved here complete with the stone pavement bearing chariot tracks.

Here the street name changes to Corso Cavour.

11 Castelvecchio and Ponte Scaligere
The castle is on the right and beyond it is the bridge.

Opposite the castle gate, Via Roma returns you to your starting point at Piazza Bra.

what to see

Excursion: The Valpolicella Region

The mountainous landscape surrounding the deep-cut valleys of the Fumane, Negrar and Marano Rivers north of Verona is home to some of Italy's most popular wines. Among its vineyards are villas, prehistoric sites, extraordinary fossils, and a host of natural attractions.

Ponte di Veja

Wine aficionados can sample the product at both modest little operations and at wineries whose names are recognised all over the world. Pedemonte is a good base for exploring (*see pp170–1*).
Ufficio Turistico Valpolicella, Viale Ingelheim 7, San Pietro in Cariano. Tel/fax: (045) 770 1920.

Molina Parco delle Cascate
A whole series of waterfalls drop from the Medieval village of Molina, in the Fumane Valley. Trails from the town pass a mill and an old dairy before following the wooded brook past the falls. The route begins at the **Museo Botanico della Lessinia**, helpful in identifying the many indigenous plants in the park (*Tel: (045) 7720 145. Open: daily Apr–Sept 9am–7.30pm, Oct–Mar Sat–Sun 9.30am–4pm*). *Vivere Molino, Via Bacilieri 1. Tel: (045) 772 0185. www.cascatamolina.it*

Museo Preistorico e Paleontologico
Paleontology and prehistory are so much a part of this fossil-laden region, where Europe's oldest rock art has been found, that this museum is a good starting place. Along with a 70 million years' old, 7m (23ft) long shark, the museum has an astonishing collection of artefacts of local prehistoric peoples.

Pza dalle Bona, Sant'Anna d'Alfaedo. Tel: (045) 532 656. www.lessiniamusei.it Open: mid May–mid Sept Tue–Sun 9.30am–12.30pm & 3.30–6.30pm, mid Sept–mid May Wed, Sat, Sun 10am–noon & 3–5pm.

Ponte di Veja

Follow the unnumbered road north from Negrar, through Fane, following signposts to Giare and Ponte di Veia. Europe's largest natural bridge, Ponte di Veja once formed the entry to a cave where prehistoric people lived. An aboriginal house is replicated at the park entrance. A short walk leads past the top (which you can cross) and down under the arch, which is 29m (95ft) high, 6m (20ft) wide and spans a distance of 50m (164ft). Human artefacts from 100,000 years ago were found here, and its geologic history reaches back more than 4 million years. *Admission free.*

San Giorgio

Follow the unnumbered road north from Dant Ambrogio di Valpolicella to San Giorgio. The church is at the top, in the village centre. The Longobard Romanesque church of **Pieve San Giorgio** and the town clustering around it atop a steep hill, are built from the stone that was carved away to flatten the hill top. Behind the church and open even when the church is not, is a gem of a cloister, tiny but perfectly proportioned, with some original carved capitals. Inside the church are rare 8th-century Longobard features.

Villa Mosconi-Bertani

It is a rare privilege to stand surrounded by frescoes in such near-perfect, original condition as those in the central hall of Villa Bertani. Built by a follower of Palladio, the neo-classical villa stands amid the vineyards it has made famous. Bertani's wines, among the most sought-after Valpolicella labels, are sold in a wing of the villa. Tastings include foods and a visit inside the villa, or tours are offered without tastings, both by prior booking.
Novare (Negrar). Tel: (045) 601 1211. Open: Mon–Fri 9am–noon & 2–6pm, Sat 9am–noon.

Villa Rizzardi

The 18th-century villa, also a premier winery, has particularly fine Italianate and English gardens. Designed in the late 1700s by Luigi Trezza, the highlight is a garden amphitheatre enclosed by clipped hedges.
Negrar. Tel: (045) 721 0028. www.guerrieri-rizzardi.it. Open: Apr–Oct Tue–Wed 3–7pm, Thur–Sun 11am–7pm.

Cloister of Pieve San Giorgio

Mantova

Surrounded on three sides by the Mincio River, which widens into a series of lakes here, Mantova is an elegant old city, and an easy one to visit. While it does not overwhelm with its number of sights, it offers one extravaganza – a palace of several hundred rooms, decorated by some of the Renaissance's greatest artists.

Ufficio Informazioni, Pza Mantegna 6. Tel: (0376) 328 253. Fax: (0376) 363 292. www.aptmantova.it. Open: Mon–Sat 9am–12.30pm & 2–6pm, Sun 9am–12.30pm.

Basilica Sant'Andrea

Piazza Sordello

THE GONZAGA FAMILY AND THEIR PALACE

The sprawling palace of the Gonzaga family dominates the Piazza Sordella much as the family dominated the city. The massive structure extends along one entire side of the piazza and for blocks behind it. Inside are more than 500 rooms and acres of gardens.

The Gonzaga family came to power in 1328 when Luigi Gonzaga ousted the ruling Bonacolsi family, establishing a line that lasted until 1707. Luigi became Captain General and Imperial Vicar of the Holy Roman Empire, gaining the title of Marquess for the family. In 1530, the family became the Dukes of Mantova in reward for the exceptional service that Francesco II had performed for the Holy Roman Empire in its struggle with Venice. In the mid-16th century, Ferrante Gonzaga, a military leader, was responsible for the enlargement of Castello Sforzesco in Milan. Great soldiers and strong rulers, the Gonzaga were also patrons of the arts, enhancing Mantova and their own palace by commissioning works of talented artists. The marriage of Isabella d'Este to Francesco II accelerated the family's patronage of the arts. The 16th-century saint, Aloysius Gonzaga, who gave up his rights of inheritance to become a Jesuit, died while ministering to plague victims on the eve of his ordination.

Starting with the palace they had wrested from the Bonacolsi, the Gonzaga began a steady building process which eventually covered much of ancient Mantova. Room after room, garden after garden the palace grew, and the finest artists and artisans were engaged to beautify it. Pisanello was brought in to decorate a room with paintings of Medieval court life. Thought to be lost, these were rediscovered in 1972. In the Sala degli Specchi (Hall of Mirrors) the very first operas were performed by Claudio Monteverdi. In one room, nine Flemish tapestries based on drawings of Raphael hang, and in the Apartment of the Metamorphoses, the walls were decorated by Giulio Romano. The Apartment of Dwarfs is exquisitely crafted, but to the scale of 0.9m (3ft) adults.

In 1390, the family built the large Castello San Giorgio to control the adjacent waterways, and in 1470 Ludovico II adapted the castle as his residence. Inside, in the Camera degli Sposi (Newly-weds Room), are frescoes by Mantegna. *Pza Sordella. Tel: (0376) 382 150. Open: Tue–Sun 9am–6.30pm, last admission 5.30pm. Admission charge.*

Federico II Gonzaga's Palazzo Te

what to see

Basilica di San'Andrea
With the building of this church in 1472, architect Leon Battista Alberti is said to have brought the Renaissance to Mantova. The interior is baroque in flavour, with coffered vaulted ceilings and an 80m (262ft) high dome. In the first chapel on the left, among paintings from his school you will find the tomb of the artist Mantegna. Other highlights are a fine baptistery and the Strozzi tomb dating from 1529.
Pza Mantegna. Tel: (0376) 328 504. Open: daily 7.30am–noon & 3–7pm.

Casa di Rigoletto
As with Juliet's house in Verona, this 15th-century house has little to do with Verdi's opera character, although a nice bronze statue in the garden brings him vividly to the scene. At one time, open-air performances of *Rigoletto* were performed here. It is now home to the city's association of tour guides.
Behind the Duomo off Pza Sordello.

Duomo
Opposite the Palazzo Ducale, the baroque facade of the cathedral is

The Baroque facade of the Duomo

matched by a fairly simple baroque interior, all designed by Giulio Romano in the 16th century as a veneer to cover a Romanesque structure.
Pza Sordello. Tel: (0376) 320 220. Open: daily 7am–noon & 3–7pm.

Palazzo Te

Once outside the city, Federico II Gonzaga's palace is now inside it. This excellent example of Renaissance Mannerism was designed by Giulio Romano in the 16th century as a place where Federico could meet up with his lover, Isabella Boschetti. The first-floor rooms are filled with exciting frescoes executed by Romano, a student of Raphael. The Sala di Psiche (Psyche's Room) is exceptional with themes of bacchanalian excess, as is the Sala dei Giganti with its towering giants and falling columns. Two museums are now housed in the *palazzo*: the Averbi collection of Egyptian artefacts and the Mondadori Fund collections of 19th-century and later paintings.
Viale Te. Tel: (0376) 323 266. Open: Mon 1–6pm, Tue–Sun 9am–6pm. Admission charge.

Rotunda San Lorenzo

This little 11th-century church was lost and presumed destroyed until the buildings that had surrounded it were taken down in 1908. The oldest church in the city, it is now restored. Its circular interior has an inner ring of Romanesque columns supporting a women's gallery (in early churches women were not allowed in the main part of the church, but a balcony was often added for them), and the walls

Torre Orologio

bear remnants of 12th- and 13th-century frescoes. The *piazza* outside is a popular meeting place, the scene of the Thursday market, and many festivals are held here. Be sure to notice the magnificent terracotta facade on the building diagonally in front of it.
Pza Erbe. Open: daily 10am–noon & 2.30–4.30pm.

Torre Orologio

Another charming feature of Piazza delle Erbe is the 1473 astrological clock, in a tower topped with a small temple. The tower is attached to the 13th-century **Palazzo Ragione** by a covered stair that leads to an upper chamber. The chamber, open only for expositions, has excellent 13th-century frescoes.

The Risorgimento and the Red Cross

The Second War of Italian Independence in 1848 pitted Austria, as the occupying power in Lombardy, against the French and their allies, a force of Sardinia-Piedmontese led by Victor Emmanuel II. The Austrian army was defeated at Magenta on 4 June 1859 and withdrew to the east. Unknown to them, their opponents moved in the same direction. Neither army knew where the other was.

The sides were fairly evenly matched in number, almost 250,000 men in all. Early on 24 June 1859, the rearguard of the Austrians and the advance guard of the Franco-Italian forces met and clashed. The battle was in the plains at the foot of the hills that rise at Solferino. Each army was uncertain of the numbers or positions of the other, and they fought in bloody and furious battles throughout the day. Late in the day the Franco-Italian force broke through the Austrian lines and the latter began to withdraw.

In that one-day battle, the Austrians lost 14,000 killed and wounded and 8,000 missing or taken prisoner. Of the French and Piedmontese, there were 15,000 killed or wounded and 2,000 missing or taken prisoner. Dead and wounded men littered the fields of Solferino and there was no one to care for the wounded or to bury the dead. Neither side made any significant effort to help those who had fallen on the field of battle. The cost of the battle was so high that Emperor Napoleon III called for a Conference at Villafranca, which resulted in a truce between the two forces.

Another result of the battle, however, was of more lasting significance to the whole world. After the battle, a Swiss citizen, Jean-Henri Dunant, was appalled by the suffering of the wounded left lying on the battlefield. He organised emergency medical assistance for the wounded, and a group of people to bury the dead. In 1862, Dunant wrote his memoirs, *Un Souvenir de*

Solferino, about the battle and its aftermath. In it he proposed that all countries join to form an emergency relief organisation. The first of these began in 1864, rapidly expanding to other countries around the globe.

Solferino was the birthplace of the International Red Cross and its Muslim equivalent, the Red Crescent. On a hillside in Solferino stands the solemn **La Capella Ossuario**, a monument to the fallen and an icon to the wastefulness of war. Behind the altar, thousands of skulls from the fallen look down upon those who come and pray. Below the chapel, the **Museo Storico** is a memorial to the fallen in the cause of Italian Independence, containing material on the battle of Solferino. *Pza Ossuaria, Solferino. Tel: (0376) 854 019. Both open: Tue–Sun 9am–noon.*

Ossuario: free admission. Museo: admission charge.

On the hill above Solferino, the **Monumento della Croce Rossa**, which memorialises Dunant and the Red Cross, is a simple promenade of trees with a monument at the end. Beside the monument is a wall of stone plaques upon which are carved the names of all nations who participate in the Red Cross's voluntary humanitarian work. The monument and its grounds were fully restored in 2003 by Austrian volunteers. Standing guard above it all is the **Rocca di Solferino**, a stone tower built in 1022 and used by the Italian forces as an observation point.

Opposite: Capella Ossuario
Above: Wall of nations at Red Cross monument

what to see

Driving Tour: Along the River Mincio

The Mincio is not a very long river, flowing only a distance of about 50km (30 miles) as the crow flies, on its way from Lake Garda to join the Po south of Mantova. Parklands follow its banks, some of which are also nature reserves that protect the wetlands and marshes nourished by the river. No road follows the meandering waters far, but several country roads cross it. One could spend a pleasant day getting lost among these roads, crossing and recrossing to discover the many faces of this river.

Associazione Turistica Colline Moreniche del Garda, Pza Torelli 1, Solferino. Tel: (0376) 854 360/001. www.dsmnet.it/collinemoreniche
Allow 1.5 hours driving time.

Begin at Peschiera, on the southern shore of Lake Garda.

1 Peschiera
The Mincio River flows out of Lake Garda, past the fortifications that guarded this important port (*see p125*).

Ponte Visconteo

Leave Peschiera on Via Secolo over the railway line, then go straight across the intersection on to Via Salvi and continue south, following signs to Ponti sul Mincio. Stay on the same road through Ponti and do not cross the river in Monzambano, but continue south, following signs toward Volta Mantovana. After about 3km (1.5 miles), turn left (east) at the crossing signposted to Valeggio. On arriving in Vallegio, turn right, then right again before the bridge.

2 Borghetto
Once devoted to silk manufacture, which harnessed the rushing Mincio to power its mills, the village was abandoned when the mills closed. Yet recent restoration has given the village new life. Cafés and craft studios fill the buildings that sit picturesquely

what to see

overlooking the water. As a backdrop, crossing the wide river is the impressive old fortified **Ponte Visconteo**. Guarding the entrance to Valeggio since 1393, its upper arches now stand in romantic partial ruin.
Carry on over the Ponte Visconteo, turning left at the end, then go right, following signs to Valeggio and the castle.

3 Valeggio

Castello Scaligeri overlooks the bridge, as well as the town below. On clear days you can see sweeping views north to the Dolomites. *Castle open: daily during daylight hours. Tower open: Sun & holidays 9am–noon & 2.30–7pm. Admission charge to tower.*

In the valley below is **Parco Giardino Sigurta**, in the former grounds of a villa that was commandeered by Napoleon as his headquarters. Now a park of 50 hectares (1,125 acres) it is so expertly landscaped into flower, topiary, herb and water gardens that it has been listed among the most beautiful gardens in the world. View it on foot, by bicycle, rented golf cart or by a 7km (4 mile) train line. *Tel: (0456) 371 033. www.sigurta.it Open: daily Mar–Nov 9am–6pm. Admission charge.*

Saturday is market day in Valeggio, and an antiques market is held on the fourth Sunday of each month. *Turismo. Tel: (0457) 951 880. www.valeggio.com. For restaurants: www.info-valeggio.it. Go south on S-249, through Roverbella until its intersection with S-62, where you turn right, following signs to Mantova.*

4 Mantova

The Mincio widens into three lakes as it flows past Mantova. The area along the north shore, west of Mantova is all part of the **Parco del Mincio**, and large stretches of the riverbank are protected as nature reserves. Excursion boats touring the three lakes are docked on the Viale Mincio, behind the palace.
***Motonaves Andes**, Pza Sordello 8. Tel: (0376) 322 875. www.amerigo.it/ANDES*

Shopping

Think of shopping in Milan, and fashion immediately comes to mind. Although few can afford the showrooms of the Quadrilatero della Moda, these are prime streets for window shopping. Big name designers are found on Via Della Spiga, with eye-catching window displays and high prices.

Stained glass at Vetroe, in Orta San Giulio

More affordable clothes are available from the shops along Corso Buenos Aires or Via Torino, aimed at a younger clientele. Even more budget-friendly are the shops which line Corso Vittorio Emanuele.
Most Milan stores open: Tue–Sat 9.30am–7.30pm, Mon 3.30–7.30pm.
Smaller shops and those outside the centre open: Tue–Sat 9.30am–12.30pm & 3.30–7.30pm, Mon 3.30–7.30pm.

Accornero
Everything for the well-dressed home.
Via Ponte Vetro 17. Tel: (02) 8909 6297.

Battistoni
Men's shirts, with fragrance ironed in.
Via della Spiga 2. Tel: (02) 794 643.

Coin
Everyday items at everyday prices.
Pza Cinque Giornate. Tel: (02) 5519 2083.

Giorgio Armani
Designer jeans to home decor.
Via Manzoni 31. Tel: (02) 7231 8600.

La Rinascente
Moderately priced department store.
Pza del Duomo. Tel: (02) 885 21.

Trussardi
Expensive leather accessories.
Via Sant'Andrea 5. Tel: (02) 7602 0380.

Discount designer outlets

Designer fashions can be found in outlets and consignment shops holding last year's lines, overstocks, returned items and samples with 50 to 70 per cent off the retail price.

Bettina Stock
Discounts of 50 to 70 per cent.
Via Simone d'Orsenigo 3.
Tel: (02) 5411 6292.

Eivissa
Discounted leather goods and furs.
Viale Monza 38. Tel: (02) 284 7954.

I Santi
An outlet located at the factory.
Via B Corio 2. Tel: (02) 5416 981. Open:
Mon–Fri 8.30am–12.30pm &
1.30–5.30pm. Metro: Porta Romana.

Le Firme A 4 Soldi
Top brands near San Bablia metro.
Galleria De Cristoforus 3.
Tel: (02) 7601 8289.

Te'Con Amiche
Consignments and samples near Piazza San Bablia.
Via Visconte di Madrone 33.
Tel: (02) 7733 1506.

Markets

Markets shouldn't be confused with artisans' fairs where original works are sold by the makers, or with antique markets. Milan has a full schedule of street markets, listed in the free paper, *Hello Milano*, which is distributed at the tourist office. A Saturday morning market is held at Viale Papiniano, near the Porta Genova metro stop.

Crafts

Outdoor artisans' fairs offer unique original works at direct-from-the-artist prices. Artisans' studios are often found on the side streets of lakeside resort towns, with exquisite work at prices far lower than those in the shops. The mountain towns of the Valle d'Aosta are known for woodcrafts.

Candle Art
Hand-sculpted candles – you can watch the artist making them!
Borgo Garibaldi 3, Bardolino.
Tel: (045) 621 0975.

Da Mastro Geppetto
Wooden wares by a master artisan.
Via Bougeois 1, Cogne (Valle d'Aosta).
Tel: (0165) 749 156.

IVAT
Wrought iron, baskets and woodcarving.
Rue Dr Grappein 32, Cogne (Valle d'Aosta). Tel: (0165) 743 22.

Les Amis du Bois
A cooperative of master woodcarvers.
Fraz. Villes Dessus 9, Introd (16 km from Aosta). Tel: (0165) 955 57.

Vetroe
Stunning, original art glass.
Via Bersani 34, Orta San Giulio.
Tel: (0322) 905 555.

Antiques

Serious collectors go to the antiquaries behind Sant'Ambrogio along via Santa Marta and Via Lanzone. On Via San Giovanni you'll find shops that specialise in one type of antique. Regular antiques markets are found at:

Como: throughout central streets, last Saturday of each month.
Desenzano del Garda: first Sunday of each month except January and August.
Mantova: third Sunday of each month.
Milan: Naviglio Grande canal, last Sunday of each month.
Milan: Piazza Diaz (near Duomo), last Saturday of each month.
Milan: Via Fiori Chiari (Monte Napoleone), third Sunday of each month.
Verona: Piazza San Zeno, third Saturday of each month (*Orange bus No 31, 32 or 33 from Castelvecchio*).

Il Collezionista
Various small antiques and furniture.
Via Carlo Alberto 3, Monza.
Tel: (039) 323 258.

Como

Como is a major silk manufacturing centre, so save buying scarves, shawls or men's neckties for here. Prices are very low, especially compared to those of the Galleria shops. Bellagio has several smart shops selling fashions, art and antiques, although these tend to reflect the moneyed clientele of the chic resort.

Martinetti
Silk manufacturer's retail outlet.
Via Torriani 41, Como.
Tel: (031) 269 053. Open: Tue–Fri 8am–noon, 2.30–6pm, Mon 2.30–6pm, Sat 8am–noon.

Verona

Via Mazzini is the main street for chic shops, and these spread into the streets adjoining it. Around Verona and Lake Garda you will find colourful ceramics made in Nove de Bassano.

Entertainment

As the unquestioned entertainment capital of Northern Italy, Milan has a busy calendar of everything from grand opera (*see pp156–7*) and celebrity performances to avant-garde cinema and underground bands. The free *Hello Milano* publication, available at the tourist office, has a complete listing.

Puppeteer in Mantova

Classical and semi-classical
Teatro Dal Verme
Concert theatre near Castello Sforzesco.
Via San Giovanni sul Muro 2.
Tel: (02) 2940 9724.
Sala Verdi, Conservatorio
Concert hall hosting well-known philharmonic orchestras.
Via Conservatorio 12.
Tel: (02) 6698 6956. www.soconcerti.it

Popular
Teatro Manzoni
Artists performing selections from their current albums.
Via Manzoni 42. Tel: (02) 7600 023.

Concert venues
Alcatraz
Big groups, usually Italian and European, play here – Exodus, Nuclear Assault.
Via Valtellina 25. Tel: (02) 6901 6352.
FilaForum
Major venue for international stars – David Bowie, Placebo and the like.
Via G Di Vittorio, Assago (shuttle bus from the Famagosta Metro station to the Fila Forum in Assago).
Tel: (02) 5300 6501.

Magazzini Generali
Doubling as a dance club, this venue runs the gamut of music road shows.
Via Pietrasanta 14. Tel: (02) 5521 1313.

Clubs
As with sophisticated clubs in any city, you need to know which night to go. The club that is head banging on Tuesday may hip hop on Thursday, with a correspondingly different clientele. Some clubs won't have room for you if you are not dressed smartly. They have their reputations to maintain as the places to see the *bella gente* ('beautiful people').

Many clubs use a card, punched for every drink, and then you pay as you leave. Admission charges may include one drink. All drinks – hard or soft – are usually the same price. Clubs are empty until near midnight, closing around 4am. Most are closed in July and August.
Blue Note
Jazz soloists in an intimate setting.
Via Borsieri 37. Tel: (02) 6901 6888.
Divina
Pure Milano-style decor with alcoves that give the illusion of walking into paintings, and toned down disco music.

directory

Teatro Dal Verme

Via Molino delle Armi at Via della Chiusa. Tel: (02) 5843 1823.

G Lounge
A Milan DJ chooses music to please G's fashion-world clientele.
Via Larga 8 (near Duomo).
Tel: (02) 8053 042.

Gavi Cafe
The decor is entertainment enough.
Via Aselli 7. Tel: (02) 7012 3136.

Hollywood
A dance club in the La Brera neighbourhood that has managed to stay *au courant* since the 1980s.
Corso Como 15. Tel: (02) 6598 996.

Jumpin' Jazz Ballroom
Traditional jazz for dancing, with live quartet.
Viale Monza 140 (upstairs).
Tel: (344) 3112 926.

La Banque
Popular disco with happy hour Fri.
Via Porrone 6. Tel: (02) 8699 6565.

Le Biciclette
Modern art, contemporary and experimental music.
Via Torti at Conca del Naviglio.
Tel: (02) 5810 4325.

Propaganda
Navigli district disco with occasional live shows; primarily student clientele.
Via Castelbarco 11. Tel: (02) 5831 0682.

Scimmie
Beside the canal in Navigli, with nightly live blues and jazz.
Via Ascanio Svorza 49.
Tel: (02) 8940 2874.

Cinema
Cineteca, Spazio Oberdan
Regular programme of films in English.
Viale Vittorio Veneto 2.
Tel: (02) 7740 6300.

Festival del Film di Locarno
Major outdoor film festival.
Pza Grande, Locarno (Lake Maggiore).
Open: mid August.

Verona
Verona's Roman arena hosts a prestigious opera festival (*see pp156–7*) each summer, along with rock and other concerts.

Teatro Romano
At least one summer Shakespeare production takes place here, and a number of dance performances, concerts and ballet.
Regaste Redentore 2. Tel: (045) 806 6485.
www.comune.verona.it

Piazza dei Signori
Summer jazz in a Renaissance setting.
Tel: (045) 806 6485.
www.comune.verona.it

Street chess game in Locarno

Opera, Opera Everywhere

Opera may have a high-brow status elsewhere, but in Italy it still enjoys wide popularity. So wide, in fact, that arias are common background music in shops and it is not unusual to hear mobile phones ringing with the opening bars of *La Donna e Mobile*.

The first stop for any opera lover in Milan is La Scala and its museum. Under major reconstruction and restoration, the great theatre has been closed for some time, and will be for an indeterminable future. Yet the show must go on, and does so in the modern Teatro degli Arcimboldi. Fans are divided in opinion: for many, the hall lacks ambience and character, but others appreciate its larger size and greater flexibility of seating. Its inconvenient location on the northern edge of the city is partly solved by shuttle buses from Piazza Duomo.

Likewise, La Scala's museum has moved to temporary quarters in the beautifully restored Palazzo Busca opposite Santa Maria della Grazie (*see pp44–5*).

Verona's Roman arena is the scene of one of Europe's major opera festivals each summer, an annual event for more than 80 years. Five operas are performed in rotation from the end of June through August in the open amphitheatre.

Nearly every Italian city of any size has a theatre where opera is performed, and many have resident companies. In addition to seeing opera performances, travellers in Northern Italy can visit sights associated with operas and the composers who wrote them.

Composer Gaetano Donizetti was born in a very modest house at Via Borgo Canale 14 in Bergamo, and although his circumstances changed with the success of his music, he remained in his home town. The Museo Donizettiana, where many of his operas were written, is in his home (*see p96*). In Santa Maria Maggiore, the nearby basilica, his marble tomb has an honoured setting, and even now fresh flowers are still left there by grateful music lovers.

Giuseppe Verdi lived in Milan and died in the Hotel Grand et de Milan on

Via Manzoni in 1901. As word of his fatal illness spread, people began to gather in silent vigil under his window, and straw was spread on the street below to quiet the sound of passing carriages. Verdi and his wife are buried in the Casa di Riposo per Musicisti (*Piaza Buonarroti 29*), a home for retired musicians that Verdi founded.

The region provided inspiration and settings, as well. Giuseppe Verdi composed *La Traviata* at Villa Margherita Ricordi in Cadenabbia, on Lake Como. Rossini composed several arias inspired by the gardens at Villa Pliniana in Torno, where he was a house guest. Verdi chose Mantova as the setting for his opera *Rigoletto*, and a statue of the jester stands in a courtyard opposite the palace of the fictional duke who caused all the trouble.

Arena di Verona
Piazza Bra 28, Verona. Tel: (045) 805 1811. Ticket sales: Via Dietro Anfiteatro 6/b. Tel: (045) 800 5151. Fax: (045) 801 3287. www.arena.it

Rosetum
Opera, sometimes in concert format. *Via Pisanello 1, Milan. Tel: (02) 4009 2015.*

Teatro alla Scala
Teatro degli Arcimboldi, Viale dell'Innovazione (shuttle bus from Pza Duomo). Tel: (02) 7200 3744. Ticket sales: Museo della Scala. Metro: Duomo (follow AIM signs). Or by telephone (in English). Tel: (02) 860 775. www.teatroallascala.org

Opposite: Poster for *Aida* performance
Above: Costume at the La Scala museum
Below: Statue of Rigoletto in Mantova

Children

Many of the things that Milan does best – shopping, art museums and historic churches – may leave children cold. However, they will warm to the lakes, especially Garda, with its perpetual holiday atmosphere.

Play area in a café

Although not every place is suitable for all ages, the most child-friendly places in Milan are the Duomo roof (*see pp28–9*), the armour collections at Castello Sforzesco (*see pp26–7*) and Teatro delle Marionette (*Via degli Olivetani 3. Tel: (02) 469 4440*). Older children may enjoy the many working models in the Museo Scienza e della Tecnica, although most signs are in Italian (*see p36*). When all else fails, head for one of Milan's many *gelato* counters.

Instead of trying to fit children into a Milan itinerary, it is better to make quick work of the city and head for more fertile ground. Castles are always a good bet, and there's a fine one as close as Angera (with a doll museum). The highest concentration of castles is in the Valtenesi, west of Lake Garda (*see p124*), although Macesine and Sirmione have good ones, too.

Nearly every lake has either swinging cable cars or a creaking funicular to a mountain top: Mottorone at Stresa (*see p55*), Monte Baldo at Malcesine (*see p119*), San Salvadore at Lugano (*see p71*) and Brunate at Como (*see p82*). Older kids will get a kick out of the quirky free transportation museum at Ranco, where they can walk under the tracks to see how a funicular works (*see p23*).

Boat rides on any of the lakes are a diversion, especially on the tiny boats that shuttle to islands: Isola Comacina (*see pp86–7*), Isola San Giulio (*see pp67–8*), Monte Isola (*see p105*) and the Borromean Islands (*see pp56–7*).

Natural wonders in the area are especially exciting for children because they involve cave people, dinosaurs and rivers doing amazing things. Cascada di Varone (*see p123*) and the Orrido di Bellano (*see p88*) are both chasms carved by waterfalls, Ponte di Veja is a huge natural arch where prehistoric people lived (*see p143*) and at Rovereto there are entire dinosaur tracks (*see pp130–31*). Roman sites (*see pp12–13*), particularly those where gladiators fought, as they did in Verona's arena, are good for children old enough to have heard of the Romans (*see p132*).

Most towns have children's parks somewhere – Riva del Garda has a good one near the castle. Bright plastic slides and climbing jungles, swings, often little cars or even a mini-train, as in Aosta, provide a place to find playmates (children don't care if they don't speak the same language). Sometimes outdoor cafés will have a couple of plastic cars on springs to occupy young minds while parents sip an espresso.

directory

Festivals will always have children's activities and are colourful, lively occasions with bands playing. Having a child with you is your ticket to join in the festivities instead of remaining an onlooker.

If you run out of distractions, consider the Hollywood-style amusement parks, the largest of which is Gardaland. This sprawls on forever, with plenty of rides and games. Don't go on weekends though or you will spend most of your time in queues (*S-249, Peschiera. Tel: (045) 644 9777. www.gardaland.it*).

One last word: Don't be distressed when someone calls your son a *bimbo* – it means 'little boy'.

Gardaland, an amusement park in Peschiera

directory

Sport and Leisure

With all the water and mountains, there are sports for all interests. Tourist offices can provide information on instructors, sports centres and equipment rentals for nearly every sport, as well as hiking guides and maps.

Sailing on Lake Maggiore

Bungee jumping
If you seek mid-air thrills, head for the north end of Lake Garda.
Paolo Fazi, Lungolago Sabbioni, Riva. Tel: (0464) 520 822.

Football (Soccer)
Milano is home to two top-flight football teams that use the same stadium. The **AC Milano** is one of the very first, founded in 1899. The other team, **Inter**, was formed in 1908. Together they provide the Milanese with a rivalry so intense that neighbours won't speak to each other. Twice a year they clash at the stadium in the San Siro district. *Stadio Giuseppe Meazza, Via Piccolomini 4 west. Tel: (02) 4042432. It is best to get tickets at: AC Milan Point, Via San Gottardo 2, Piazza XXIV Maggio. Tel: (02) 89422711. Open: Mon–Sat 10am–7.30pm. Inter Ticket One/Spazio Oberdan, Viale Vittorio Veneto. Tel: (02) 2953 6577. Open: Tue–Sun 10am–9pm.*

Golf
Lombardy offers a wealth of opportunity for golfers, with 35 nine- or eighteen-hole courses, nine promotional courses and nine practice locations. Be sure to call for guest status and to reserve time. Most courses are open all year.

Lake Como: Golf Club Villa d'Este has an 18-hole course, among Europe's most challenging par 69 courses, 7km (4 miles) from Como. *Via per Cantu 13, Montorofano. Tel: (031) 200 200. www.villadeste.it. Open: Mar–Dec. Closed: Tue.*
Golf Club Menaggio e Cadenabbia, on the west side of the lake, is an 18-hole, par 70 course, 40km (25 miles) from Como. *Via Golf 12, Grandola ed Uniti. Tel: (0344) 321 03. www.menaggio.it. Open: Mar–Nov.*
Lake Garda: Arzaga Golf Club is an 18-hole par 72 course, southwest of the lake and 25km (15.5 miles) from Brescia, 65km (40 miles) from Verona. *Carzago di Cavagese Della Riviera. Tel: (030) 680 6266. www.palazzoarzaga.com*
Gardagolf Country Club has three nine-hole courses, par 35–6, 30km (18.5 miles) from Brescia, 65km (40 miles) from Verona. *Via Angelo Omodeo 2, Soiano Del Lago. Tel: (0365) 674 707. www.gardagolf.com. Closed: Mon.*
Lake Iseo: Franciacorta Golf Club, an 18-hole, par 72 course, 20km (12.5 miles) west of Brescia. *Via Provinciale 34/B, Nigoline di Corta Franca. Tel: (030) 984 167. Email: franciacortagolfclub@libero.it Closed: Sept–May Tue.*
Lake Lugano: Golf Club Lanzo is a nine-hole, par 37 course, 16km

directory

161

(10 miles) from Lugano and 30km (18.5 miles) from Como. *Via Pian Nel Noci, Lanzo d'Intelvi. Tel: (031) 839060. Email: glflanzo@tin.it. Open: Apr–Nov. Closed: Mon.*

Milan East: Molinetto Country Club is an 18-hole, par 71 course, 10km (6 miles) from Milan. *Strada Statale Padana Superiore 11, Cernusco Sul Naviglio. Tel: (0292) 105 128. Email: molinetto.c.c@ntt.it. Closed: Mon.*

Milan North: Golf Club Milano in Monza has an 18-hole and a 9-hole course, par 72–36, 18km (11 miles)

Boat rentals in Limone sul Garda

from Milan. *Via Mulini San Giorgio 7, Parco di Monza. Tel: (039) 303 0812. www.golfclubmilano.it. Closed: Mon.*
Milan South: Golf Club Le Rovedine, 18 holes, par 72, only 4km (2.5 miles) from Milan. *Via Karl Marx 18, Noverasco di Opera. Tel: (0257) 606 420. www.rovedine.com. Closed: Mon.*
Milan West: Green Club Lainate, 18 holes, par 71, 10km (6 miles) from Milan. *Via A. Manzoni 45, Lainate. Tel: (0293) 710 76. www.golf-hotel.it*

Horse riding
Centro Ippico Tenuta la Torre takes you out into the hills and mountains around Lake Como, welcoming all levels of expertise and with English-speaking guides (*Tel: (0348) 894 7814/008 0869. Yellow signs between Menaggio and Porlezza. Bus: line C12*). At the south end of the lake, near Como, you can ride from a 13th-century farm in the fields and woods around tiny Lake Montorfano with **Circolo Ippico Il Grillo** (*Via Chigollo 7, Capiago Intimiano. Tel: (031) 462 219*). Itineraries run from an hour to a full day, and at all levels of difficulty. English and Western saddles are available at both places.

Mountain biking
With so many mountains, there is a lot of territory to explore. At the northern end of Lake Garda, **Nautic Club Riva** has a team of guides and instructors for riders of all levels. Tours are half- or full-day (*Viale Rovereto 44, Riva. Tel: (0464) 552 453. www.nauticclubriva.com*). **Marco Segnana Surf Centre** also has mountain bike rentals (*Foci del Sarca, Torbole and Lungolago dei Pini 19, Riva. Tel: (0464) 505 963. www.surfsegnana.it*). For street bikes, go to **Fiori E Bike** (*Viale Tigli 24, Riva. Tel: (0464) 552 453. www.pederzolli.it*), or **Carpentari Bike Shop** (*Via Matteotti 16, Torbole. Tel: (0464) 505 500. www.carpentari.com*). On Lake Como, rent from **Cavalcario Club** (*Guello de Bellagio. Tel: (031) 964 814*).

Sailing and boating
On all but the smallest lakes you will find plenty of rental boats of all varieties. Ask for *barca* (boat), *barca a vela* (sailing boat), *motoscafo* (motorboat). Put these together with *noleggio* (for hire) and you will be on the water before you know it. Because of the predictable winds, the northern end of Lake Garda is among one of the best places to sail. **Club Nautica Riva** rents both catamarans and sailboats, and their instructors can teach both beginners and advanced sailors (*Viale Rovereto 44, Riva. Tel: (0464) 552 453. www.nauticclubriva.com*).

Canoeists on the north end of Lake Garda should go to Paolo Fazi at Lungolago Sabbioni for hourly, half-day and full-day rentals of single and double boats (*Tel: (0464) 520 822*).

Swimming
Along all the lakes look for small *piscina* (pool) or *spiaggia* signs. Don't expect broad sandy beaches – most are stony or made of gravel, so you will need a blanket or heavy towel. Many cities and towns have swimming pools that are open to travellers as well as to locals.

directory

In Riva, **Piscina Enrico Meroni** (*Via Martini 25. Tel: (0464) 520 078*) and **Riva Sport Centre** (*Viale dei Tigli 40. Tel: (0464) 552 072. Admission charge*).

Windsurfing

Some of Europe's prime windsurfing waters are at the northern end of Lake Garda. Light winds in the mornings and stronger afternoon winds provide varied challenges, especially good for learners. **Nautica Club Riva** has qualified instructors and rental equipment (*Viale Rovereto 44, Riva. Tel: (0464) 552 453. www.nauticclubriva.com*). Waters off Torbole, just a few kilometres from Riva, are the best.

Marco Segnana Surf Centre is a large and professional facility with instruction and rental on a beautiful beach (*Foci del Sarca, Lungolago dei Pini 19, Torbole and Lungolago dei Pini 19, Riva. Tel: (0464) 505 963. www.surfsegnana.it*).

Cycling in the Gran Paradiso National Park, Val d'Aosta

Food and Drink

Milan is known for its excellent restaurants, largely because the Milanese often dine out, and demand quality. Fashionable city hot spots and some restaurants elsewhere can be expensive, but you will find reasonably priced restaurants everywhere.

Farmhouse cheeses

That is not to suggest that you should avoid the dining establishments, often in villa hotels, where creative chefs have gained a name for themselves. These restaurants offer a chance to sample the artistry of some of Europe's finest chefs, and it would be a shame to miss out on such a experience. You will need to book well ahead for any of these, especially on a weekend. For those in villas, it is often more economical to book a room with dinner (*see pp176–7*).

A *trattoria* usually has a more limited menu and lower prices than a *ristorante* (both terms mean 'restaurant'), and frequently the waiter will describe the day's specials in place of a menu. An *osteria* is a wine bar that serves snacks and sometimes a few dishes. A *pizzeria* is normally a restaurant that specialises in wood-oven pizzas. That said, the terms are used interchangeably and a *trattoria* may be fancier and pricier than the *ristorante* next door, and the *osteria* may be a chichi, rustified country inn. If in doubt, ask to see a menu (generally posted at the door). For home-style cooking, look for signs advertising *cucina casalingua*. For a sandwich, go to a bar or café.

A typical meal includes a *primo* (first course) of *pasta* (pasta) or *risotto* (rice).

A *secondo* (main course) often includes only the meat or fish, and perhaps a small serving of vegetables. Vegetables (*contorni*) and salads (*insalate*) are usually ordered separately. *Dolci* (sweets) follow. *Antipasti* are small dishes that precede the pasta course. Although Italians may progress through all these courses, this does not mean you need to. Ask about the size of the pasta serving to determine how many courses to order, since handmade *ravioli* tends to be far lighter than a *penne* or *linguini* dish.

If breakfast (*colazione*) is not included in the accommodation price, cafés are better value than hotels. Coffee with hot milk – *cappuccino* or *caffè latte* – is only drunk at breakfast. Coffee ordered at any other time of day will automatically be *espresso* unless you request *caffè americano*.

REGIONAL DISHES

Milan's speciality dishes are *cotoletta Milanese* (veal cutlet) and *risotto*, a creamy rice dish incorporating anything from porcini mushrooms to seafood. On the lakes and in Verona, *polenta* is a favourite – a maize porridge often served with porcini. *Ossobuco*, braised veal shins, is a heartier rustic dish. Lake fish are abundant, usually grilled or pan-fried. Vegetables fresh from nearby farms are used in season, so you may find every restaurant offering artichokes or asparagus at the same time.

RESTAURANTS

Hours are generally noon to 2.30pm or 3pm, and 7pm to 10pm or later. Italians usually arrive at about 8pm. Most restaurants in Milan close for the whole month of August. Tip waiters about 5 per cent over the included service charge (*coperto*).

Meal prices
Prices at Italian restaurants can vary widely in price. You will find everything from value-for-money finds to five-star dining blowouts. Prices in this guide are subject to fluctuation and should only be used as a rough guide.

*	Under €60
**	€60–€80
***	€80–€100
****	Over €100

Aosta
La Cave de Tillier Ristorante Brasserie*
Gnocchi fonduta – tender potato pasta in a creamy fontina cheese sauce – is a speciality.
Via de Tillier 40. Tel: (016) 523 0133.

Ristorante Praetoria*
The rabbit is excellent, as are the cheese-filled *ravioli*.
Via San Anselmo 9.
Tel: (0165) 443 56.

Artisanal linguini for sale

Bergamo (Città Alta)
Caffè del Tasso*
The best café location in town, with good pastries and a piano bar.
Pza Vecchia 3. Tel: (035) 237 966.

Da Franco Ristorante*
Lively, informal setting for well-prepared local dishes, including *caprese* salad of mozzarella and tomatoes.
Via Colleoni 8. Tel: (035) 238 565.

Mangili Angelo
Shop here for foods to take home: local cheeses, salami, ham, dried pasta and ingredients for the local *polenta*.
Via Gombito 8.
Tel: (035) 248 774.

Taverna dei Colleoni**
Upmarket restaurant noted for *casoncelli*, the local meat ravioli.
Pza Vecchia 7.
Tel: (035) 232 596.

Taverna della Taragna*
Hidden behind a cheery bar, this traditional *trattoria* has no menu, prodigious portions, and *polenta* worthy of sainthood.
Viale Papa Giovanni XXIII 3, San Pellegrino.
Tel: (0345) 215 64.

Trattoria Tre Torre*
Polenta with porcini and Taleggio cheese is a local speciality.
Pza Mercato del Fieno (Via San Lorenzo). Tel: (035) 244 366.

Lake Como
Albergo Ristorante Il Vapore*
Homemade dishes and perfectly cooked lake fish.
Pza T Grossi 3, Mennagio.
Tel: (0344) 322 29.

directory

Falchetto***
Terrace dining with panoramic views; booking recommended on weekends.
Salita Peltrera 37 (on road to Brunate). Tel: (031) 336 5000.

Il Solito Posto**
Delicate asparagus *ravioli* or hearty *ossobuco* in a cosy atmosphere.
Via Lambertenghi 9, Como. Tel: (031) 271 352.

Ristorante Hosterietta**
A good selection of creamy *risotto* combinations, from white truffles to red chicory.
Pza Volta 57, Como. Tel: (031) 241 516.

Ristorante Silva**
Family-owned, serving simple dishes of fresh lake fish and house pasta.
Via Carcano 12, Localita Loppia, Bellagio. Tel: (031) 950 322.

Lake Garda

Bar Pizzeria Adria*
Excellent *bruschetta* and light dishes served in an olive-tree shaded garden, overlooking Il Vittoriale.
Via Caduti 17, Gardone Sopra.

Pizzeria La Strambata*
Lively place for creative pizzas and generous *caprese* salads.
Via Fosse, Bardolino. Tel: (045) 721 0110.

Ristorante Gardesana**
Regional dishes served, such as delicate white lake fish – *lavarello*.
Pza Calderini 20, Torre del Benaco. Tel: (045) 722 5411.

Trattoria La Biocca*
Pumpkin-filled *ravioli* is the house speciality.
Vicolo Molino 6, Desenzano. Tel: (0309) 143 658.

Caprese salad combines tomatoes with buffalo mozzarella

Villa del Sogno***
Dinner here is a fine art, from the creative concepts to the beautiful presentation and service.
Via Zanardelli 107, Gardone Riviera.
Tel: (0365) 290 181. www.villadelsogno.it

Lake Lugano
Ristorante Locanda Orico*
The *degustazione* menu offers six courses; the carpaccio is outstanding.
Via Orico 13, Bellinzona.
Tel: (091) 825 1518. www.locandaorico.ch

Trani**
Smart wine bar with delectable game and vegetarian dishes. Sample Ticino wines here.
Via Cattedrale 12, Lugano.
Tel: (091) 922 0505.

Lake Maggiore
Il Sole di Ranco*
One of the finest dining experiences in Northern Italy; this chef richly deserves his two Michelin stars.
Pza Venezia 5, Ranco (Angera).
Tel: (0331) 976 507. www.ilsolediranco.it

La Bruma del Lago*
Serves lake fish and interesting pasta variations in a post-modern setting.
Corso Mazzini 65, Belgirate.

Locanda dei Mai Intees**
Simply the most delectable lamb you'll ever eat; the pasta chef is a genius.
Via Nobile Claudio Riva 2, Azzate (Varese). Tel: (033) 245 7223.
www.mai-intees.com

Ristorante Belvedere*
An airy vine-draped terrace above the lake; try tender *tortellini* filled with goat cheese.
Via Piave 11, Ranco. Tel: (0331) 976 609.

Restaurant tables in the street

Milan
Café Dell'Opera**
Expensive if you take a table, but a very elegant place for *gelato* or a pastry (*pasta*).
Via Manzoni 12, Milano.
Tel: (02) 799 653.

Café Sarducci*
Café near Sant'Ambrogio, good bar snacks in late afternoon.
Via San Vittore 2. Tel: (02) 890 0440.

Café Vergnano 1882*
Excellent pasta dishes and sandwiches. The dining room is in the back.
Via Speronari 3 (near Duomo).
Tel: (02) 8699 6858.

Dining rooms overlook the water in every lake town

Da Ilia**
This restaurant has been here for half a century, so it must be doing something right.
Via Lecco 1. Tel: (02) 2952 1895.
www.ristorante-ilia.it

Joia**
Inspired vegetarian dishes and fish.
Via Panfilo Castaldi 18.
Tel: (02) 2952 2124. Closed: weekends, Aug, Dec and Jan.

La Carbonella***
Look for *risotto* with white truffles from nearby Alba.
Via Torraggio 9. Tel: (02) 861 833.

Pizzeria di Porta Garibaldi**
Their own *gnocchi* (potato pasta), and pizza served by the slice.
Corso Como 6. Tel: (02) 655 1926.

Trattoria C'era Una Volta**
A rare restaurant in Milan that serves traditional *ossobuco*.
Via Palermo 20. Tel: (02) 654 060.

Trattoria Il Carpaccio*
The kind of unpretentious restaurant you always wish for in a city and rarely find; superb *tortellini*.
Via Palazzi 9 (opposite Hotel Sanpi).
Tel: (02) 2940 5982.

Trattoria Milanese**
Typical Milanese dishes, including *ossobucco*.
Via Santa Marta 11. Tel: 02 8645 1991.

Monza

Derby Grill***
Don't be misled by the British name; this is fine Nuovo-Italian dining. Bookings essential.
Hotel de Ville, Via Regina Margherita 15.
Tel: (039) 382 581.

Ristorante Toscano Trepiedde**
Hospitable, informal, with Tuscan menu.
Viale Lombardia 2, Rondo di Monza.
Tel: (039) 360 265.

directory

Verona
Due Torre***
Impeccable service in a former *palazzo*; dishes include *risotto* with pignoli (pine nuts) and gorgonzola sauce, or lamb chops with mixed wild berries.
Piazza Sant'Anastasia 4.
Tel: (045) 595 0444.

Le Petarine*
Osteria serving homemade seasonal specialities like tripe soup.
Via San Mamaso.
Tel: (045) 594 453.

Osteria del Duca*
Local favourite for pasta and vegetable dishes, veal carpaccio with arugola, and snails with *polenta*.
Via Arche Scaligere 20.
Tel: (045) 594 474.

Osteria Sgarzerie*
Traditional eatery serving savoury *ossobuco alla Milanese*.
Corte Sgarzerie. Tel: (045) 800 0312.

Ristorante Arquade***
Choose the market tasting menu (a menu based on what is in the market that day), with accompanying wines, to sample the breadth of this brilliant chef's talents and the scope of the villa's famed wine cellars.
Villa Del Quar, Via Quar 12, Pedemonte (Valpolicella).
Tel: (045) 680 0681.
www.hotelvilladelquar.it

Ristorante Greppia**
Summer dining on the *piazzetta* (small piazza); pasta stuffed with pumpkin, and hard-to-find Venetian dishes.
Vicolo Samaritana 3 (off Via Mazzini). Tel: (045) 800 4577.

Trattoria alla Colonna*
Polenta served with trout, cod or rabbit.
Largo Pescheria Veccia 4 (near Scaligeri tombs).
Tel: (045) 596 718.
Open: until 2am.

Trattoria alla Pigna**
Creative dishes such as steelhead trout with a brandy and courgette flowers sauce; the menu is translated.
Via Pigna 4. Tel: (045) 800 0492.

The daily menu is usually posted outside

Savouring Local Wines

The soils of Lombardy and the neighbouring regions of Piedmont and Veneto are perfect for wine production. Deep, sweet calcareous earth is drenched with plenty of sunshine and enough water to produce the best wine grapes. Long known for their good, reliable wines, vintners have recently become more sophisticated, creating even finer wines while retaining the unique essence of these lands. Local connoisseurs were quick to appreciate this, and the better local restaurants have wine lists that run to pages of such wines. Even in neighbourhood *trattorie*, the *vino di tavola* (house wine) served by the carafe (*vino sfuso,* literally 'loose' or from the barrel) is almost certain to be of a high quality.

From the Piedmont, west of Milan, look for the Barbaresco, Barbera d'Alba and Barolo reds, and Gavi or Roero Arneis whites. From the eastern shores of Lake Garda come the hearty Bardolino and the lighter Valpolicella, both reds. From Soave, just east of Verona, come delicate and light whites. The vineyards of Lombardy produce the dry red Botticino and Cellatica, and the softer and more perfumed Gropello. Capriano del Colle is pressed in both a red and a white.

Franciacorta in Lombardy, south of Lake Iseo, has one of the newest and most exciting DOC (*denominazione di origine controllata,* or registered domaine) regions. Look for the words *Franciacorta DOCG* (the 'G' stands for 'guaranteed') on the labels of sparkling wine. The strict rules of DOCG limit production – they require that grapes are placed into small containers, that only chardonnay or pinot blanc grapes are used, and that the wine is produced by secondary bottle fermentation only. Look also for the equally carefully made *DOC Franciacorta* whites – straw coloured, dry and velvety – and the DOC reds, which are vivid in colour, and fruity.

Tourist offices often have brochures identifying wineries in each region, and many have wine trail maps. Use these or watch for the signs to direct you to a winery that offers tastings in their *cantina* (cellar). In some wine shops you can view the winemaking process, but you won't find the whole neighbourhood 'treading' the grapes now that the process is mechanised. Some of the more prestigious wineries ask that you phone ahead since they prepare food to accompany a tasting and even – like the outstanding Bertani winery in Novare – arrange for you to tour the interior of the villa (see p143). Expect to pay based on the type of experience – more for a formal tasting than for a drop-in *cantina*.

WINE BARS

A good way to sample a variety of local wines is at a wine bar – *enoteca* or *osteria* – where a wide selection is served by the glass. These establishments usually also offer a board of local artisan cheeses, a good accompaniment to wines of the same *terroir* (growing environment). These generally open late afternoon or early evening and close between midnight and 2am.

Enoteca Segreta
Vicolo Samaritana 10, Verona.
Tel: (045) 801 5824.

Lostrano Bar
Via Adamo del Pero 8, Como.
Tel: (031) 249 429.

Monti's Café
Via A Volta 47, Azzate (Lake Varese, near Maggiore). Tel: (0332) 458 583.

Osteria del Gallo
Via Vitani 20, Verona.

Osteria Panesalame
Via Marocco 22, Riva del Garda.
Tel: (0464) 551 954.

Opposite: Valpolicella grapes ready for harvest
Above: Roadside sign advertising wine for sale
Below: Local wines at a sidewalk market

Hotels and Accommodation

Milan has some of Italy's classiest and best-designed hotels, while overlooking the lakes are the grand resort hotels and historic villas (*see pp176–7*), as well as plenty of attractive, smaller hotels.

Hotel Capello D'Oro in Bergamo

A hotel in Italy is usually just that – a building with corridors of guest rooms, usually with a restaurant. Beyond that, designations are less clear. A small *albergo* may resemble a *locande*, although the latter is usually a nice country home turned into an inn.

One way to assure a level of quality is to book through affinity groups (these differ from hotel chains) such as Best Western, The Charming Hotels, Relais & Chateaux or SRS. These are independently-owned, have joined hotels with equal standards, and directories and websites with photographs. Italy's own star system helps, and is based on regular inspections. You can expect two-star hotels to have private bathrooms, three-star to have in-room telephones and television. Internet points are still uncommon.

When staying in Milan, consider location since some neighbourhoods are unsavoury after dark. One such area is around Stazione Centrale, but the many good hotels there are convenient for those arriving by train or air. Using taxis after dark is not a bad idea anywhere in the city.

Establish the rate when reserving a hotel room, and request fax or e-mail

HOTEL GROUPS

Best Western

www.bestwestern.it
Australia (1 800) 222 422
Ireland (800) 709 101
New Zealand (09) 520 5418
South Africa (011) 339 4865
UK (0 800) 393130
USA (1 800) 528 1234

The Charming Hotels

www.thecharminghotels.com
UK (0 800) 2427 6464

SRS Hotels

www.srshotels.com
Australia (1 800) 553 549
South Africa (011) 339 4865
New Zealand (0 800) 447 555
UK (0 800) 7779 6753
USA/Canada (1 800) 223 5652

Relais & Chateau

www.relaischateaux.com
UK (0 800) 2000 00 02
USA/Canada (1 800) 735 2478

confirmation. Always have confirmed bookings for August (except in Milan, which is nearly empty then), Easter week and for arrival and departure nights. Some lake hotels close from November to March.

HOTELS
Aosta
Hotel Europe
Very attractive hotel in the historic centre (you can walk to major sights and the railway station), with accommodating staff, and covered parking.
Pza Narbonne, 8, Aosta 11100.
Tel: (0165) 236 363. Fax: (0165) 405 66.

Bergamo
Best Western Premier Cappello D'Oro
Freshly decorated, and in the centre of the lower city, near railway and funicular stations; covered parking. Full English breakfast buffet.
Viale Pappa Giovanni XXIII 12, Bergamo 24121. Tel: (035) 232 503.
Fax: (035) 242 946. www.bestwestern.it

Hotel Agnello d'Oro
High in the old city, charming, comfortable and only steps away from all the sights.
Via Gombito 22, Bergamo 24121.
Tel: (035) 249 883. Fax: (035) 235 612.

Lake Como
Grand Hotel Tremezzo Palace
Freshly restored to original Belle Epoque splendour. Directly on the lake, it is backed by beautiful gardens. Outstanding breakfast buffet.
Via Regina 8, Tremezzo.
Tel: (034) 440 446. Fax: (034) 440 201.

Grand Hotel sign in Stresa

Terminus
Freshly renovated Belle Epoque grand hotel on the main piazza at the boat landing.
Lungo Lario Trieste, Como.
Tel: (031) 329 111. Fax: (031) 302 550.

Lake Garda
Albergo Alighieri
In the old town centre, studio apartments on a pedestrianised street.
Via Dante Alighieri 48, Bardolino 37011.
Tel: (0457) 211 988. Fax: (0456) 228 283.

Grand Hotel Gardone
Art Deco on a grand scale, the hotel sits alongside the lake.
Via Zanardelli 84, Gardone Riviera 25083. Tel: (0365) 202 61.
Fax: (0365) 226 95. www.grangardone.it

Hotel Alpi
Comfortable modern rooms, on the main highway, an easy walk to town.
Campograngé, Malchesine 37018.
Tel: (0457) 400 717. Fax: (0457) 400 529.

Guest room at Il Sole di Ranco

Hotel Capri
Contemporary rooms with balconies. Convenient location for activities.
Via Mirabello 21, Bardolino 37011.
Tel: (0457) 210 106. Fax: (0456) 212 088.
www.hotel-capri.com

Hotel Europa
Recently (and beautifully) redesigned, in the centre of town, overlooking the boat landing, clock tower, dining and shopping.
Pza Catena 9, Riva 38066.
Tel: (0464) 555 433. Fax: (0464) 521 777.
www.rivadelgarda.com/europa

Hotel Garni Diana
Modern and bright hotel with a pool, a short downhill walk to the lake.
Via Scoisse 8, Malcesine 37018.
Tel: (0457) 500 192. Fax: (0457) 400 415.
www.malcesine.com/diana

Hotel Piroscafo
A family-run hotel on the harbour, newly renovated.
Via Porto Vecchio 11, Descenzano 25015.
Tel: (0309) 141 128. Fax: (0309) 912 586.

Hotel Vittorio
Art deco hotel with bright, pleasant rooms, most with balconies. Stunning lake views. Situated in the town centre, and has covered parking.
Via Porto Vecchio 4, Descenzano 25015.
Tel: (0309) 912 245. Fax: (0309) 912 270.

Lake Lugano
Hotel de la Paix
Balconies overlook the lake and mountains. You can walk to the Paradiso boat stop, train and funicular stations.
Via Cattori 18, Lugano 6900 (Switzerland). Tel: +41 (091) 960 6060.
Fax: (091) 960 6066. www.delapaix.ch

Lake Maggiore
Best Western Hotel Milano
Very attractive hotel with friendly staff, on the lake with dockage and terrace restaurant.
Via Sempione 4, Belgirate-Novara 288 32.
Tel: (0322) 765 25. Fax: (0322) 76295.
www.bestwestern.com

Best Western Villa Carlotta
Large lake shore villa with fine gardens and attractive rooms with internet points; often hosts large coach groups.
Via Sempione 121/125, Belgirate, 28832.
Tel: (0322) 764 61. Fax: (0322) 767 05.
www.bestwestern.com

Grand Hotel des Iles Borromees
One of Northern Italy's most renowned luxury hotels, situated in a lush park overlooking the islands.
Lungolago Umberto, Stresa.
Tel: (0323) 938 938. Fax: (0323) 324 05.

Milan
Antica Locanda Leonardo
Small inn with excellent central location, congenial owners and parking.

Corso Magenta 78, Milano 20123.
Tel: (02) 4801 4197. Fax: (02) 4801 9012.
www.leoloc.com

Grand Hotel Duomo
Upmarket rooms overlook the Duomo; the only hotel on Piazza Duomo.
Via San Raffaele 1, Milano 20123.
Tel: (02) 8833. Fax: (02) 8646 2027.
www.grandhotelduomo.com

Hotel Ariston
Modern, comfortable and ecologically sound – air is ionised and bicycles are available.
Largo Carrobbio 2, Milano 20123.
Tel: (02) 7200 0556. Fax: (02) 7200 0914.

Hotel Mediolanum
Attractive contemporary hotel, exceptionally well managed. Near the Stazione Centrale.
Via Mauro Macchi 1 (at Via Napo Torriani), 20124 Milano.
Tel: (02) 670 5312. Fax: (02) 6698 1921.
www.mediolanumhotel.com

Hotel Sanpi Milano
Newly renovated, upmarket rooms, each unique. The charming courtyard is a rare oasis, a short walk from Stazione Centrale.
Via Lazzaro Palazzi 18, Milano 20124.
Tel: (02) 2951 3341. Fax: (02) 2940 2451.
www.hotelsanpimilano.it

Hotel Pierre
Plush and convenient – all automated utilities in the room are controlled by one button.
Via de Amicis 32, Milano 20123.
Tel: (02) 7200 0581. Fax: (02) 805 2157.

Art Deco Hotel Vittorio in Descenzano del Garda

Hotel Spadari al Duomo
A few steps from Piazza Duomo, the Euro-modern rooms are decorated by notable Italian artists.
Via Spadari 11, Milano 20123.
Tel: (02) 7200 2371. Fax: (02) 861 184.
www.spadarihotel.com

Verona
Due Torre Hotel Baglione
A beautifully maintained palace furnished with period antiques, each room unique. Impeccable service.
Pza Sant'Anastasia 4, Verona 37138.
Tel: (045) 595 0444.

Hotel Aurora
Newly renovated rooms, terrace bar overlooks the market.
Pza Erbe, Verona 37138.
Tel: (045) 594 717/597 834.
Fax: (045) 801 0860.

Hotel Mazzanti
Simple and clean, situated on the main shopping street.
Via Mazzini 6, Verona 37138.
Tel: (045) 800 6183. Fax: (045) 801 1262.

Living in a Villa

The next best thing to owning your own villa with a view over an Italian lake is to be a guest in someone else's. This is quite possible, since the owners of many of these historic villas have turned them into small hotels, nearly always with a notable restaurant.

Villas are smaller and more personal than hotels. Their architecture is distinguished, each room different in its shape, furnishings, decor and character. The villas are usually the hosts' ancestral home; you really are a guest in a private home. Most of all, each has a history, often of several hundred years, and living at one gives you a glimpse of those past centuries.

The setting might be in a village or leafy neighbourhood of a small city, in gardens on the lake shore or surrounded by the villa's own vineyards. The dining rooms are in the hands of highly rated chefs with awards and stars to their honour. Most villas also have distinguished wine cellars.

Il Sole di Ranco

Elegant rooms are styled in soft colours, with full-length windows overlooking gardens and Lake Maggiore. The villa's vine-draped terrace is the place to watch the sunset reflected in the lake's waters. Day begins with breakfast breads baked in the villa's highly praised restaurant.
Pza Venezia 5, Ranco 21020 (Varese). Tel: (0331) 976 507. Fax: (0331) 976 620. www.ilsolediranco.it

La Villa, Hotel De La Ville

A distinguished former private home adjacent to the deluxe boutique hotel, the villa is a secret hideaway behind its fence. Breathtakingly elegant rooms, rich in architectural detail, are furnished with fine art and antiques. Every amenity is remembered, including a small TV screen beside the bathroom mirror, and a private lounge downstairs for villa guests.
Viale Regina Margherita 15, Monza 20052. Tel: (039) 382 581. Fax: (039) 367 647. www.hoteldelaville.com

Locanda dei Mai Intees

On the dining room walls there are Medieval frescoes discovered during the restoration of the manor, which was built in the 1400s. Rooms are decorated in rich Renaissance colours and antique furnishings, but the stylish marble baths are strictly 21st century. Hospitable owner Carla Promati's heart is in the villa's kitchen, and it shows.
Via Nobile Claudio Riva 2, Azzate 21002 (Varese). Tel: (0332) 457 223. Fax: (0332) 459 339.

Villa del Quar

The noble wine estate, surrounded by Valpolicella vineyards, is an Italian National Monument. When *torchieres* (large holders for torches used on the outside of buildings) and other historic details of their Renaissance ancestral home have needed replacing, the owners have commissioned handmade replicas. The airy guest rooms are a seamless blend of antique detail and mod cons, and the terrace café looks out at a clover-shaped swimming pool at the edge of a vineyard.
Via Quar 12, Pedemonte 37020 (Verona). Tel: (045) 680 0681. Fax: (045) 680 0604.www.hotelvilladelquar.it

Villa Del Sogno

In its own hillside park of exotic trees, this Art Nouveau villa looks down over the lake. The spacious terrace is the size of a village *piazza*, a good place to enjoy an evening aperitif or the outstanding breakfast buffet. There are matching suites of richly inlaid furniture in the guest rooms.
Via Zanardelli 107, Gardone Riviera 25083. Tel: (0365) 290 181. Fax: (0365) 290 230. www.villadelsogno.it

Opposite: Guest room in La Villa, Hotel de La Ville in Monza
Above: Terrace of Villa Del Sogno in Gardone Riviera

Practical Guide

Arriving
Entry requirements
EU citizens can enter Italy for an unlimited stay with a valid passport. US, Australian, Canadian and New Zealand passport holders must have passports that are valid for at least three months from the entry date for up to 90-day stays without a visa. Reasonable amounts of tobacco, alcohol and personal belongings are allowed tax-free.

By air
Two large airports serve Milan. Linate (*Tel: (02) 7485 2200*) is near the city and Malpensa (*Tel: (02) 7485 2200*) is halfway between Milan and Lake Maggiore – a good starting place for the lakes. Express buses connect Malpensa with at least one city on each major lake. Both airports are connected to the city centre by regular transport. *Linate. Bus: No 73 to San Babila metro. Malpensa. Express trains and buses to Stazione Centrale train station.*

By rail
Milan's Stazione Centrale railway station is on the M3 (yellow) metro line, four stops from Piazza Duomo. Trains to Lakes Como, Maggiore and Garda leave from this station. There is a taxi rank just outside the station; the minimum charge of about €3 increases at night, on holidays, and for luggage. The Stazione Centrale area is not the best place to wander around at night.

Camping
Camp sites, found all over the lakes region, are most plentiful around southern Lake Garda (*www.gardacamp.com*). Most are barely larger than a caravan, although a few sites are more suitable for a camping holiday, such as the park-like **3Lago Camping** on tiny Lago di Ghirla, between Lakes Maggiore and Lugano (*Via Trelago 20, Ghirla (Varese). Tel: (0332) 716 383. www.3lagocamping.com*). In Milan, Campeggio Città di Milano offers tent pitches and sports facilities (*Via Airaghi 61. Tel: (02) 4820 0134. Metro: De Angali, then bus no. 72*). Tourist office accommodation directories usually list camp sites.

Italian trains run on time

Children

Italians, as a rule, adore children and though they do not often travel with their own, they are highly tolerant of other people's. Bring child car seats to avoid the extra charge many car rental companies add – if they are available at all. Hotels and accommodation usually supply a baby cot or roll-away bed if asked when booking.

Milan is difficult for parents of infants and toddlers because of the stairs in metro stations; and you must collapse pushchairs on trams and buses. However, locals will be quick to help. Only an occasional restaurant will have high chairs – best to tuck a collapsible seat into the pushchair pocket. (*See pp158–9.*)

Climate

The Alps to the north of the region moderate summer heat (although it is still hot), while the lake waters moderate the winters. Mountain-sheltered western shores have created mild micro-climates where tropical plants grow, north of their usual range. While showers are common in spring, autumn and winter, snow accumulations on the lake shores are rare. Sunshine averages three to four hours daily in winter and more than nine in summer. Summer is brutally hot in Milan and the Po Valley; winters (December to February) surprisingly cool, with snow, fog and rain.

Consulates
Australia
Via Borgogna 9. Tel: (02) 7770 4217.
Canada
Via Vittor Pisani 19. Tel: (02) 675 81.
New Zealand
Via Guido d'Arezzo 6. Tel: (02) 4801 2544.
South Africa
Via San Giovanni sul Muro 4. Tel: (02) 809 036.
UK
Via San Paolo 7. Tel: (02) 733 001.
USA
Via Principe Amadeo 2/10. Tel: (02) 290 351.

Crime

Pickpockets, purse-snatchers and car thieves are the biggest safety worry for travellers in Northern Italy, especially in Milan. But the number of police in Stazione Centrale shows how seriously the city authorities take their recent crackdown. Keep handbags and cameras in your hand or hidden, never hanging loose. Savvy women do not carry handbags at all, stowing guidebooks and personal effects in a tote, and keeping

MILAN
Average Rainfall for year 1084mm (43in)
Average Temperature for year 12°C/53.6F

Weather Conversion Chart
25.4mm = 1 inch
°F = 1.8 × °C + 32

money, documents and credit cards in a hidden wallet. Men should also use hidden wallets, and never carry one in a rear pocket that can be easily slit from the bottom.

Lock cars and hide tourist items, such as maps or guidebooks, so that thieves won't assume there to be luggage in the car boot. If a robbery does occur, report it immediately to the police, to support insurance claims. Carrying identification, such as a passport, is required by law.

Driving
Car hire
Book car hire well in advance since cars are seldom available without a reservation. The lowest rates are frequently in a package with air fare, booked through the airline. Often, you must purchase the collision damage waiver insurance cover, which is not included in Italy, adding another expense to car hire. If you live outside Europe, you can avoid this by leasing a car. Renault Eurodrive has a very smooth system for this, completing the paperwork in advance and meeting you with a brand-new car at Milan airport. Rates compare favourably with rentals (and without added VAT), and drivers over 70 are not banned, as they are by most rental agencies. *Renault Eurodrive. US (800) 221 1052. www.renaultusa.com. France (0) 505 1515.*

Documents and insurance
EU and US drivers need only their own current driving licence; other travellers should also carry an International Driving Permit, obtained in your own country, usually through an automobile club. You must have registration and insurance documents in the car at all times. It is also important to get a card from your insurer to prove that you have third-party coverage.

Driving conditions
The main east–west motorway (*autostrada*) is the A-4 between Milan and Venice, which passes close to the cities in this book and to the shore of Lake Garda. Once you overcome your initial horror at the way Italian drivers weave between cars at high speeds, the A-4 is not unlike motorways anywhere. More disconcerting are the winding, narrow mountain roads, often with precipitous drops and no guard rails. Don't be surprised to meet cars rounding tight corners at least halfway across your lane. Stay alert and defensive, eyes on the road at all times,

Euro banknotes and coins

and avoid these roads in rain, winter and at night.

Finding your way
Route numbers are not always on road signs, so look for signposts pointing to towns and cities on your route. It is important to know the destination city of an *autostrada* in each direction, since the motorways are not labelled by compass points. A-26 to Lago Maggiore is signposted to Gravellona, a tiny town at the Swiss border. This system can be quite puzzling when trying to determine which *autostrada* entrance to take.

When asking directions, watch as well as listen to the reply, since directions will all be accompanied by helpful hand gestures. *Sempre dirrito* means 'straight ahead' and *semaforo* is a traffic signal light. *Segnale* is a signpost and *rotatoria* is a roundabout.

Breakdowns and accidents
If you have a breakdown, pull over if possible, and place a warning triangle 100m (388ft) behind the vehicle (or post a passenger with waving arms). Then dial 116 for assistance or flag down another driver with a mobile phone. The tow truck driver will probably not speak English, but will have a multilingual auto parts manual. You will have to pay for towing and parts. Members of automobile clubs in their own country can usually arrange for cover; ask your local automobile club about a letter of introduction or ETI booklet.

In the event of an accident, remain at the scene until police arrive, stay calm and request an English-speaking interpreter before making a statement.

Filling up at a petrol station

Fuel
Petrol (unleaded is *benzina senza piombo*) and diesel are sold by the litre. Many stations are self-service, using credit cards at the pump, but some smaller stations require cash. Be sure to keep your tank full on weekends, since many stations close then.

Right-hand driving
In Italy, all traffic drives on the right, which is a problem for those from the UK and other left-hand drive countries. The most difficult moments are when you start out each day, especially if you enter a road or street without traffic. Solve this by using some sort of sign to alert you each time you enter the car.

Traffic regulations
The left lane of an *autostrada* is only for passing and other vehicles must keep to the right. If a driver approaching from behind in the same lane flashes high

beams, you are expected to move to the right as soon as you can. Do not pass on the right.

Rules at intersections and roundabouts will seem familiar, except that they are backwards for those used to driving on the left. When there is no other indication, the vehicle on the right has the right of way, except at a roundabout. There a vehicle in the circle has the right of way over entering traffic. A green arrow indicating a left turn only means that turning is allowed, not that oncoming traffic is stopped by a red light.

Speed limits
Although rarely observed by locals, the speed limit on an *autostrada* is 130km/h (80mph). Lower limits are posted when the road is dangerous or in urban areas (usually 100km/h (60mph)) or in a construction zone (*zona cantiere*), where you are required by law to slow down. In towns, the limit is 50km/h (30mph), and residential areas often post speed limits of 30km/h (20mph). The maximum speed on rural roads is 90km/h (55mph); be especially careful when these go through the centre of villages, where blind turns can hide all sorts of perils. The speed limit for caravans over 3550kg (3.5 tonnes) and camper vans is 100kph (60mph) on *autostrade*, 80km/h (50mph) elsewhere, and 50km/h (30mph) in towns.

Drinking and driving
Italy has strict laws limiting a driver's permissible blood alcohol level to 0.08 per cent. Exceed this and risk stiff penalties – as well as an accident.

A driver with an illegal level also risks being automatically held at fault in any accident.

Seat belts
Seat belts are mandatory for driver and all passengers, whether in the front or back seats. Children under 12 must be in the back seat.

Tolls
Most *autostrade* charge tolls. Normally you take a ticket at the beginning and pay at the end, using cash or a bank or credit card. Be careful to find the right exit booth, and be aware that using a credit card requires a pin number.

Electricity
Italy operates at 220 volts. UK appliances will work, but require an adaptor to the European plug with two round prongs. American appliances need a transformer and an adaptor.

Emergency telephone numbers
Police (*carabinieri*)
Tel: 112.
Emergencies (*pronto soccorso*)
Tel: 113.
Automobile Club d'Italia (ACI)
Breakdown service for road assistance
Tel: 116.
Ambulance (*ambulanza*)
Tel: (02) 3883.

Health
Public health conditions are generally good in Northern Italy and drinking water is normally safe (although many travellers prefer bottled water). No immunisations are required or necessary

for travel. Minor medical problems are usually handled by pharmacies (*farmacia*). These take turns staying open for emergencies (*normal hours: Mon–Fri 8.30am–12.30pm & 4.30–7pm*). Each pharmacy posts a sign outside telling of the nearest open pharmacy. The one on the first floor of Stazione Centrale is open 24 hours (be sure to use a taxi at night). For more serious illnesses or injury, a tourist office or hotel can suggest English-speaking doctors. Bring enough prescription medications for the entire trip, with a copy of the prescription in generic form, plus Aspirin, which is available only in pharmacies in Italy.

Insurance

Experienced travellers carry insurance to cover their belongings and cost of the trip. Travel insurance should include provision for cancelled or delayed flights, as well as immediate transportation home in the case of medical emergency. EU citizens are entitled to free emergency medical care in a public hospital. Showing a passport might be enough but you should carry a form E111 (UK travellers get one from the post-office). Non-EU citizens are only covered if they have travel medical insurance.

Lost property

Milan's *Ufficio Oggetti Rinvenuti* (Lost Property Office) holds items found in public transport or stations (*Via Friuli 30. Tel: (02) 8845 3907. Open: Mon–Fri 8.30am–4pm*). Property lost on trains is kept at Stazione Centrale, in the *Deposito Bagagli* (Left Luggage) office, next to Information. Lost passports or other documents are likely to be put into a letter box, so check at the Postal *Ufficio Oggetti Rinvenuti* (*Via Ferrante Aporti. Tel: (02) 669 0658*). To check on lost luggage call the relevant airport (*Malpensa. Tel: (02) 5858 0070. Linate. Tel: (02) 7012 4451*).

Maps

The most up-to-date and reliable road maps are published by Michelin and by Automobile Club d'Italia (ACI). It helps to have one with topography, since what looks like a short cut might go over a mountain. *Automobile Club d'Italia (ACI), Via Marsala 8, 00185 Rome. Tel: (06) 499 8234.*

Media

English-language daily newspapers are available at larger news-stands. The most useful local newspaper for travellers is *Corriere della Serra*, for its 'Milan' section listing concerts and events. Published monthly, *Hello Milano* is distributed by the tourist office, with events and museum hours, nightlife and local insider information.

Milan's public places are well patrolled by police

Language

Italian is not a difficult language. It has fewer words than many other languages, and few synonyms. Every letter is pronounced and pronunciation rules are much like English. Those who read other Romance languages, especially Spanish, will be able to read Italian. Italians are very sympathetic to foreigners who try to speak their language, and will listen patiently and appreciate your attempts. It also helps that Italians use their hands so expressively – often their sign language will carry you through when you don't understand a word. Those who deal most with travellers speak some English, but everywhere people are very pleased when you at least begin with *Buongiorno* (Good day).

LANGUAGE PRONUNCIATION

C followed by E or I	CH	
C all other times	K	
G followed by I or E	G in George	
G all other times	G in gorge	
GG	DG in edge	
ZZ	TZ (palazzo is said 'palatzo')	
GN	NY as in canyon	
GL	LL as in medallion	

NUMBERS

1	uno	21	ventuno	
2	due	22	ventidue	
3	tre	30	trenta	
4	quattro	40	quaranta	
5	cinque	50	cinquanta	
6	sei	60	sessanta	
7	sette	70	settanta	
8	otto	80	ottanta	
9	nove	90	novanta	
10	dieci	100	cento	
11	undici	101	centuno	
12	dodici	110	centodieci	
13	tredici	200	duecento	
14	quattordici	500	cinquecento	
15	quindici	1000	mille	
16	sedici	5000	cinquemila	
17	diciassette	10,000	diecimila	
18	diciotto	50,000	cinquanta mila	
19	diciannove	1,000,000	un milione	
20	venti	2,000,000	due milione	

DAYS OF THE WEEK

Monday	lunedì
Tuesday	martedì
Wednesday	mercoledì
Thursday	giovedì
Friday	venerdì
Saturday	sabato
Sunday	domenica

MONTHS OF THE YEAR

January	gennaio
February	febbraio
March	marzo
April	aprile
May	maggio
June	giugno
July	luglio
August	agosto
September	settembre
October	ottobre
November	novembre
December	dicembre

WEIGHTS

1/2	un mezzo	100gm	un etto	
1/4	un quarto	1kg	un chilo (key-low)	
1/3	un terzo			
		1 pound	mezzo chilo	
		1 litre	un litro	

directory

USEFUL PHRASES

yes/no	si/no
thank you	grazie
please	per favore
you are welcome	prego
excuse me	scusi
I'm sorry	mi dispiace
I would like	vorrei
I don't understand	non capisco
I don't like that	non mi piace
I want	voglio (vol-yo)
I would prefer	preferisco
okay	va bene
big/little	grande/piccolo
hot/cold	caldo/freddo
open/closed	aperto/chiuso
right/left	destra/sinistra
good/bad	buono/cattivo
fast/slow	presto/lento
much/little	molto/poco
expensive/cheap	caro/economico
go away (as a command)	va via!
at what time	a che ora
do you speak English?	parla inglese?
where is...?	dove...? (doh-veh)
stop it	smettila
leave me alone	lasciami in pace

DRIVING

accident	l'incidente
air pressure	la pressione
breakdown	il guasto
car	la macchina
does not work	non funziona
full	pieno
ignition	l'accensione
motor	il motore
oil	l'olio
petrol/diesel	la benzina/ il gasolio
petrol station	il distributore
straight ahead	sempre diritto
turn right/left	gira a destra/ sinistra
unleaded	senza piombo
water	l'acqua

ROAD SIGNS

attenzione	watch out
deviazione	detour
divieto di accesso/ senso vietato	no entry
divieto di sosta/ sosta vietata	no parking
incrocio	crossroads
limite di velocità	speed limit
parcheggio	parking
perícolo	danger
pronto soccorso	first aid
rallentare	slow down
senso unico	one-way street
strada chiusa	road closed
strada senza uscita	dead end, cul-de-sac
tenere la destra	keep right
traffico limitato	restricted access
uscita veicoli	exit
vietato fumare	no smoking
vietato il sorpasso	no overtaking (passing)
vietato il transito	no through traffic
zona rimorchio	tow-away zone

directory

Men's Suits							
UK	36	38	40	42	44	46	48
Rest of Europe	46	48	50	52	54	56	58
US	36	38	40	42	44	46	48

Dress Sizes						
UK	8	10	12	14	16	18
France	36	38	40	42	44	46
Italy	38	40	42	44	46	48
Rest of Europe	34	36	38	40	42	44
US	6	8	10	12	14	16

Men's Shirts						
UK	14	14.5	15	15.5	126	16.5 17
Rest of Europe	36	37	38	39/40	41	42 43
US	14	14.5	15	15.5	16	16.5 17

Men's Shoes						
UK	7	7.5	8.5	9.5	10.5	11
Rest of Europe	41	42	43	44	45	46
US	8	8.5	9.5	10.5	11.5	12

Women's Shoes						
UK	4.5	5	5.5	6	6.5	7
Rest of Europe	38	38	39	39	40	41
US	6	6.5	7	7.5	8	8.5

Money matters

The euro (pronounced 'arrow' in Italy) is the currency, and exchange facilities are near airport arrival gates; Malpensa's are open 24 hours. Avoid the cash changing machines, which charge exorbitant fees.

Avoid carrying large amounts of cash, or hide it well. Although safer, traveller's cheques must usually be cashed at banks; credit or debit cards are easier. If possible, bring at least one major credit card – Visa is the most commonly accepted. Some small businesses – agri-tourism lodgings, family restaurants and some small hotels – do not accept them, but most places do.

Cash machines (*bancomat*) have the best exchange rates and are everywhere. Check with your card issuer to find out which network to use and be sure that your PIN number can be used abroad (it should not have zeros). A bank debit card that draws directly on your account usually costs less for cash advances than a credit card, but either assures the best commercial exchange rate.

Banks are usually open *Mon–Fri 8.30am–1pm or 1.30pm*, sometimes reopening for an hour in the afternoon and staying open later on Thursday. Stock up on euros before weekends because banks are closed and cash machines may be out of money, or out of order.

Opening times

Expect all but the largest, museums, shops and offices to close at midday, although this is slowly changing. Closing times vary between noon and 1pm, and reopening is most often at 2pm or 3pm, but may be later, especially in the summer. Churches are notoriously irregular in their opening hours, but the most common hours are *9am–1pm & 3–7pm*. Smaller museums and attractions are also highly erratic, so don't be surprised if they are closed when they say they are open. Time is not an essential word in the Italian vocabulary.

Most shops close on Monday mornings. Food stores usually close Wednesday afternoons. Major city supermarkets and petrol stations on *autostrade* stay open during the middle of the day, and some Milan stores have done away with midday closing. In tourist places or during the summer, shops may remain open longer. Many businesses and nearly all restaurants in Milan close for the month of August, making it a poor time to be there.

Nearly all museums and attractions, and many churches are closed on Monday. Mondays are a good day for a driving or train tour, or to ride a mountain tramway. Cafés at the top will be open.

Police
Each town's *Polizia urbana* deals with local traffic and parking, and *Polizia stradale* handle highway traffic. Report thefts to a *questura* (police station) and ask for a *denuncia*, a document needed to file insurance claims. More serious crimes are handled by *Carabinieri* (military police).

Post offices
Most tourist maps note the location of the city's main post office (*ufficio postale*), or ask at your hotel. You can buy postage stamps (*francobolli*) from most news-stands.

Public holidays

1 January	**New Year's Day**
6 January	**Epiphany**
March/April	**Easter Monday**
25 April	**Liberation Day**
1 May	**Labour Day**
15 August	**Feast of the Assumption**
25 December	**Christmas Day**

Public transport
ATM operates the metro, buses and trams, and tickets are available at news-stands, vending machines and at kiosks in some stations. Validate your ticket in the red meter as you enter the vehicle or when going through the turnstile. If you plan to ride more than three times in a day, a day ticket is better value. It needs to be validated on first use. The metro runs until about midnight. If a bus does not replace the route, you can use the economical Radiobus until 2am to get from the city centre to the outer districts. *Tel: (02) 4803 4803.*

Milan's new streetcars

Telephones
Make calls from public telephones with a card (*carta telefonica*) bought from any news-stand. You must use the card in a phone from that company (green phones for green cards, etc), so be sure to ask where the nearest one is when you buy a card, and buy in small denominations. You must snap the corner off a phone card before using it.

Telephone numbers are still in the process of change, so if your call does not go through, check to see if a digit has been added. Ask a tourist information centre or hotel desk to help if you cannot reach a number. Always ask for the surcharge rate before making international calls from a hotel room.

You can recognise a cellular phone (which even some businesses use) by its prefix 3. Do not dial the usual 0 before it (although older publications say to). Mobile phones in Italy use the GSM European standard; US cellular phones do not work.

To call or fax Italy from outside the country, dial international access, then the country code (39), then the area code without the initial 0, then the number. To make an international call from Italy, dial the access code 00, then the country code (Australia = 61, Ireland = 353, New Zealand = 64, UK = 44, US and Canada = 1) followed by the local number, omitting the first digit if it is 1 or 0.

To access your own network to place a call from Italy, use the following direct dial numbers:

Tourist information office sign

Australia: Telstra 172 1061; Optus 172 1161.
Canada: 172 1001.
Ireland: 172 0353.
New Zealand: 172 1064.
UK: BT 172 0044; Cable & Wireless 172 054.
US: AT&T 172 1011; MCI 172 1022; Sprint 172 1877.

Time

Italy is GMT plus one hour in winter, and two hours ahead from the end of March to the end of September. Time is not an important issue in Italy, and people may be surprised when you turn up at a set time.

Tipping

Tip waiters about 5 per cent, although most Italians simply leave between €1 and €5 on the table, depending on the establishment. In family-run restaurants, tipping is not expected, but appreciated. In cafés and bars, simply leave the small change. The modest *coperto*, or cover charge at most restaurants is not for the service; in fact, no one seems sure exactly what it is for.

Toilets

Finding a public toilet can be a challenge. On the *autostrade*, petrol stations have them. You'll also find them in museums and bus and train stations (although the latter will often not be an aesthetic experience. They are labelled *Uomini* for men and *Donne* for women. Most cafés don't object if you go in just to use the toilet.

Tourist information

Most towns with any tourist traffic (or hope of it) have tourist information centres, either called *pro loco*, *APT* or *ARPT*. They are usually at the main railway or boat station, the main *piazza*, or near a popular attraction. Apart from those in large towns, these usually close at midday. Normal hours are *Mon–Sat 9am–1pm and 4–6pm or 7pm; shorter hours in winter, or closed*. Some can make accommodation reservations, and all can suggest options. Some offices offer useful booklets of detailed dining, shopping, accommodation and attractions listings, but you usually have to request these. This is the best source of current opening hours, which change often.

Travellers with disabilities

Except in the cities, where a few places have wheelchair access, facilities for mobility-impaired travellers are poor. Airports are mostly wheelchair accessible, lake steamers usually are, and major hotels have often adapted a few rooms, but travel can be very difficult otherwise. Most museums, theatres and public buildings are not ramped. However, an occasional light shines: admission to football matches is free to people with disabilities through gates 50–1. Parking is free in special blue zones for cars with an international disabled sticker. For current information, contact **RADAR**, *12 City Forum, 250 City Rd, London EC1V 8AF. Tel: 020 7250 3222.*

San Pellegrino's wide arcaded main street is accessible to all

index

A
Abbazia di Piona 88
accommodation 5, 90–1, 172–7
agri-tourism 5, 90–1
airports 18, 178
Anfo 128
Angera 52–3
Aosta 12–13, 51
archaeology
  Bergamo 96
  Como 78
  Lake Garda 124, 127, 129
  Milan 30–1
  Verona 139
architecture 32–3
Arco 122, 123
Arcumeggia 64
Arena di Verona 134, 157
Arona 54
art galleries 93, 109
art museums 26–7, 30, 36, 38–9, 135
Art Nouveau 30, 33, 100–1
Ascona 62
Aula della Curia 94

B
banks 186
Bardolino 120–1
Basilica di San Giacomo 80–1
Basilica di Sant'Andrea 146
beaches 118, 124
Bellagio 46, 80–1
Bellano 88
Bellinzona 62
Bergamo 92–7, 99
boats 22–3, 158, 162
  Borromean Islands 56–7
  Lago di Garda 113
  Lake Como 46
  Lake Lugano 72–3
Borghetto 150–1
Borromean islands 56–7
Borromeo family 60–1
botanical gardens 62–3, 114–15, 121
Brenzone 118
Brescia 12, 13, 106–11
Brissago 62–3
Brunate 46, 47, 82

C
camping 91, 178
Campione d'Italia 72
Cannero Riviera 58
Cannobio 58
Capitolium 106, 111
Capo di Ponte 103
car hire 18, 180
Casa del Manzoni 30–1
Casa di Giulietta 134–5
Casa di Rigoletto 146
Castel Seprio 64–5

Castello Drena 123
Castello Sforzesco 26–7
Castelvecchio 135
Castiglione Olona 65
castles
  Bergamo 93
  Brescia 106–7
  Lago d'Iseo 104, 105
  Lake Garda 118, 119, 122–7
  Lake Maggiore 52–3, 62
  Rovereto 130–1
  Val d'Aosta 51
  see also Castel...
cathedrals see Duomo
Ceniga 123
Centovalli 74–5
Cernobbio 82
children 158–9, 179
churches 4
  Brescia 111
  Centovalli 75
  Isola Comacina 86–7
  Lago di Lugano 71–3
  Lago d'Iseo 104, 105
  Lago d'Orta 67, 68–9
  Lake Como 76, 79, 83–4, 88–9
  Lake Garda 115, 120–1, 124, 127
  Lake Varese 65
  Mantova 147
  Milan 32–3, 39–40, 42–5
  Valpolicella region 143
  Verona 137–9
CIMAC (Civico Museo di Arte Contemporanea) 30
Cimitero Monumentale 30
Civici Musei d'Arte e Storia Santa Giulia 107, 111
Civico Museo Archeologico 30–1
climate 179
clock towers 96–7, 123, 147
Clusane 103
Cogne 51
Colleoni Chapel 94, 95
Comacina 86–7
Como 46–7, 78–9, 153
consulates 179
Contarini Fountain 96, 97
credit cards 186
crime 179–80
culture 14–15
currency 186

D
Decumanus Maximus 107
Desenzano del Garda 124
dining 164–9
dinosaur tracks 130
disabled travellers 189
drinking 164–71, 182
driving 180–2

Lake Garda 113, 128–9
Milan 18–19
Mincio River 150–1
Val d'Aosta 50–1
Duomo
  Bergamo 94–5
  Brescia 108, 110
  Como 78
  Mantova 146–7
  Milan 24–5, 28–9, 32
  Monza 48
  Salò 115
  di Santa Maria Matricolare 135

E
eating out 164–9
electricity 182
emergency telephone numbers 182
entertainment 154–7
events 14–17, 159
excursions
  Lake Como 46, 76–7
  Lake Varese 64–5
  Monza 48–9
  Rovereto 130–1
  Val Brembana 100–1
  Valpolicella region 142–3

F
families 158–9, 179
Fashion Quarter 25, 39, 152
Fenis Castle 51
festivals 14–17, 159
Fonda Toce 54
food and drink 164–71
frescoes
  Bergamo 94
  Lago di Garda 122, 127
  Lago di Lugano 71, 72–3
  Lago d'Iseo 105
  Lago d'Orta 68
  Lake Como 79, 88–9
  Lake Maggiore 53
  Lake Varese 65
  Mantova 147
  Valpolicella region 143
  Verona 139
funiculars 23, 46, 63, 71, 92–3, 158

G
Galleria Vittorio Emanuele II 34
galleries 93, 109
Gandria 72
Garda 121
Gardaland 159
Gardatrentino 122–3
gardens
  Lake Como 79, 81–2, 84–5
  Lake Garda 114–15, 121
  Lake Lugano 71, 73

Lake Maggiore 55–7, 59, 62–3
  Mincio River 151
  Verona 136
Gardone Riviera 114–15
gates 97, 139
Giardini Publici 34
Giardino Giusti 136
golf 160–2
Gonzaga family 145
governance 10
Gran Paradiso 51
Gravedona 88–9

H
health 182–3
history 8–9
horse riding 162
hotels 172–5

I
Il Vittoriale 114, 116–17
insurance 180, 183
Intragna 74–5
Iseo 104
Isola Bella 56–7
Isola Comacina 86–7
Isola Madre Gardens 56
Isola Pescatore 57
Isola San Giulio 66–7

J
Juliet cult 133–5, 139

L
La Rocca 93
La Scala 34, 156, 157
Lago Bleu 50
Lago di Garda 112–29
Lago di Ladro 129
Lago di Lugano 70–3
Lago d'Iseo 102–5
Lago d'Orta 66–9
Lake Como 46–7, 76–85, 88–9
Lake Idro 128–9
Lake Maggiore 52–63
Lake Varese 64–5
Lamberti Tower 136
language 184–5
l'Arena di Verona 134, 157
Laveno 58
Lazise 121
leisure 160–3
Leonardo da Vinci 36, 77
Liberty style 30, 33
  see also Art Nouveau
Limone sul Garda 114, 115
Limoni Riviera 114–15
lion of St Mark 98–9, 132, 136
Locarno 63, 74
Lodrone 128–9
lost property 183
Lugano 70–1
Luino 59

index

M
maestri comacini 72, 76, 79–81
Maggiore 52–63
Malcesine 118
Mantova 144–7, 151
maps 5, 183
  Bergamo 92
  Brescia 111
  Centovalli 75
  Lago di Garda 113, 128
  Lago di Lugano 70
  Lago d'Iseo 102
  Lago d'Orta 67
  Lake Como 77
  Lake Maggiore 53
  Mantova 144
  Milan 24, 41
  Mincio River 151
  trains 20–1
  Val d'Aosta 50
  Valpolicella region 142
  Verona 132, 141
Marcote 72–3
markets 59, 70, 151–3
Matterhorn 50
media 183
medical help 183
Menaggio 89
Milan 12, 18–19, 24–45, 152, 154–5
Mincio River 150–1
Molina Parco delle Cascate 142
monasteries 88, 103, 105
money 186
Monte Baldo 118–19
Monte Bianco (Mont Blanc) 51
Monte Bre 71
Monte Isola 102, 104–5
Monte San Salvadore 71
monuments 30, 148, 149
Monza 48–9
mountain tramways 23
Museo Archeologico 96, 139
Museo Civico, Como 78
Museo Civico di Scienzi Naturali 96
Museo d'Arte Antica 26–7
Museo degli Strumenti Musicali 27
Museo dei Transporti 52–3
Museo della Preistoria e Protostoria 27
Museo delle Arti Decorative 27
Museo Donizettiano 96
Museo La Scala 35
Museo Nazionale Scienza e della Tecnica 36
Museo Poldi Pezzoli 36, 41
Museo Preistorico e Paleontologico 142–3
Museo Storico Della Città 96

Museo Zucchi 36
museums
  Brescia 107
  Italian independence 149
  Lago di Lugano 71, 72
  Lago d'Orta 69
  Lake Garda 120–4, 127, 129
  Mantova 147
  Milan 26–7, 30–1, 34–6, 38–9, 41
  Rovereto 130
  Verona 135, 139
  see also Museo...

N
nature reserves 54, 129
Nesso 82–3

O
Olivi Riviera 120–1
Omegna 68
opening hours 124, 186–7
opera 34–5, 156–7
Orta San Giulio 68–9
Orto Botanica del Monte Baldo 121

P
Palazzo Bagatti Valsecchi 36–7
Palazzo Borromeo 56
Palazzo de Ragione 136
Palazzo Reale, Monza 49
Palazzo Te 145, 147
parking 19
parks
  children 158
  Lago di Garda 115, 124
  Lago d'Iseo 102–3
  Lake Maggiore 55, 59
  Lake Varese 65
  Mincio River 150, 151
  Monza 49
passports 178
Peschiera 125, 127, 150
Pettenasco 69
Piazza dei Signori 136–7
Piazza del Foro 106, 108
Piazza delle Erbe 136, 140
Piazza Loggia 109, 110
Piazza Mercante 38, 39, 40
Piazza Vecchia 96–7
Piazza Vittoria 110
Piazzetta Duomo 94–7
Pinacoteca Accademia Carrera 93
Pinacoteca Ambrosiana 38–9
Pinacoteca Civica Tosio Martinengo 109
Pinacoteca Di Brera 39
Pinoteca 27
Pisogne 105
police 187
Ponte di Veja 143
Ponte Scaligero 135

Ponte Visconteo 150, 151
post offices 187
Pre 129
public holidays 187
public transport 187

Q
Quadrilatero della Moda 25, 39, 152

R
railways *see* funiculars; trains
Red Cross 148–9
restaurants 164–9
Risorgimento 148–9
Riva del Garda 122–3
River Mincio 150–1
Rocca Borromeo 52–3
rock art 103
Roman remains 12–13
  Brescia 106–11
  Lago di Garda 124, 127
  Milan 31, 32
  Verona 132, 136, 139–41
Romeo and Juliet cult 133, 134–5, 139
Rotunda San Lorenzo 147
Rovereto 130–1

S
safety 18, 179–80
St Mark's lion 98–9, 132, 136
Salo 115
San Bernardino alle Ossa 39
San Cristo 111
San Fedele 42
San Fermo Maggiore 137
San Giorgio 143
San Pellegrino 100–1
San Pietro in Lamas 105
San Sebastiano 42
San Sepulcro 42
San Zeno Major 138
Santa Maria degli Angioli 71
Santa Maria della Grazie 44–5
Santa Maria Maggiore 75, 94, 95
Santa Maria in Organo 139
Santa Maria presso San Satiro 33, 40, 44, 45
Sant'Abbondio 33
Sant'Ambrogio 32, 42–3
Sant'Anastasia 138
Sant'Eustorgio 44
Scaligeri castles 127
Scaligeri tombs 137
Scavi Archeologici 139
shopping 152–3
Sirmione 125, 126, 127
sports 160–3
Storo 129
Strada degli Artiglieri 130
Stresa 55
Switzerland 52, 62, 70, 72

T
Teatro Romano
  Brescia 109, 111
  Verona 139, 155
telephones 182, 187–8
Tempietto di Santa Croce 95
theatres 34, 139, 156, 157
time 188
timeline 8–9
tipping 188
toilets 188
Tomba di Giulietta 139
Torno 83
Torre Orologio 147
Torri del Benaco 119
Toscolano-Maderno 115
tourist information 10, 189
trains 18, 20–1, 22–3, 46, 74–5, 178
transport 18–23, 180–2, 187
  Centovalli 74–5
  Lago di Garda 113
  Lake Como 46, 76–7
  Lake Lugano 71, 72–3
  Lake Maggiore 52–3, 63
  Verona 132–3
Tremezzina Riviera 84–5

V
Val Brembana 100–1
Val d'Aosta 13, 50–1
Valeggio 151
Valpolicella region 142–3
Valtenesi 124
Varenna 89
Varese 65
Venetian empire 98–9, 132, 136
Verdasio 75
Verdi, Giuseppe 156–7
Verona 12, 13, 132–41, 153, 155
Viale Mura 97
Villa Balbianello 84
Villa Carlotta 85
Villa Lagarina 131
Villa Melzi d'Eril 81
Villa Mosconi-Bertani 143
villa rental 176–7
Villa Rizzardi 143
Villa Serbelloni 81
Villa Táranto 59
Vini Vallagarina 131

W
walks
  Brescia 110–11
  Lake Como 81
  Milan 28–9, 40–1
  Verona 140–1
waterfalls 123, 142
weather 179
windsurfing 163
wine 120–1, 131, 142–3, 170–1

ACKNOWLEDGEMENTS

Thomas Cook Publishing wishes to thank the photographer, STILLMAN ROGERS, for the loan of the photographs reproduced in this book, to whom the copyright in the photographs belong.

Copy-editing: JO OSBORN

Index: INDEXING SPECIALISTS (UK) LTD

Maps: PC GRAPHICS, Old Woking, UK

Proof-reading: CAMBRIDGE PUBLISHING MANAGEMENT LTD and RICHARD HALL

Travellers

Feedback Form

Please help us improve future editions by taking part in our reader survey. Every returned form will be acknowledged. To show our appreciation we will send you a voucher entitling you to £1 off your next *Travellers* guide or any other Thomas Cook guidebook ordered direct from Thomas Cook Publishing. Just take a few minutes to complete and return this form to us.

We'd also be glad to hear of your comments, updates or recommendations on places we cover or you think that we ought to cover.

1. Which *Travellers* guide did you purchase?

---

2. Have you purchased other *Travellers* guides in the series?

    Yes ☐

    No ☐

    If Yes, please specify_____

3. Which of the following tempted you into buying your *Travellers* guide: (Please tick as many as appropriate)

    The price ☐

    The FREE weblinks CD ☐

    The cover ☐

    The content ☐

    Other_____

4. What do you think of :

    a) the cover design? _____

    b) the design and layout styles within the book? _____

    c) the FREE weblinks CD? _____

5. Please tell us about any features that in your opinion could be changed, improved or added in future editions of the book or CD:

Your age category: ☐ under 21 ☐ 21-30 ☐ 31-40 ☐ 41-50 ☐ 51+

Mr/Mrs/Miss/Ms/Other

Surname_____ Initials_____

Full address: (Please include postal or zip code)_____

Daytime telephone number: _____

Email address: _____

☐ Please tick here if you would be willing to participate in further customer surveys.

☐ Please tick here if you would like to receive information on new titles or special offers from Thomas Cook Publishing (please note we never give your details to third party companies).

Please detach this page and send it to: **The Editor, Travellers, Thomas Cook Publishing, PO Box 227, The Thomas Cook Business Park, Peterborough PE3 8XX, United Kingdom.**

tear along the perforation

The Editor, Travellers
Thomas Cook Publishing
PO Box 227
The Thomas Cook Business Park
Peterborough, PE3 8XX
United Kingdom